STARLIGHT AND STORM

GASTON RÉBUFFAT

STARLIGHT
AND STORM

TRANSLATED BY WILFRID NOYCE
AND SIR JOHN HUNT

JON KRAKAUER

SERIES EDITOR

Introduction by David Roberts

THE MODERN LIBRARY

NEW YORK

1999 Modern Library Paperback Edition

Biographical note copyright © 1999 by Random House, Inc.
Copyright © 1956, 1957, 1984 by E. P. Dutton & Co., Inc.
Introduction © 1999 by David Roberts
Series Introduction copyright © 1999 by Jon Krakauer

Starlight and Storm is published by arrangement with
Editions Denoel, Paris. The English translation by Wilfrid Noyce and
Sir John Hunt, with a foreword by Sir John Hunt, is published by
arrangement with Dutton Plume, a division of Penguin Putnam, Inc.

PHOTO CAPTIONS: ii, the Tour Ronde ridge of Mount Maudit;
x, climbing in the Calanques; xxxii, demonstrating the "chimneying"
technique in a chimney of medium breadth; xxxvi, in the Vallee
Blanche; xlii, on the Aiguille Mummery
PHOTO CREDITS: ii, x, xxxii, xxxvi, xlii, and 38 © Gaston
Rébuffat; 2, 68, 82, 94 © John Noble/Wilderness Photographic
Library; 110 © Jon Krakauer

LIBRARY OF CONGRESS CATALOGING-IN-PUBLICATION DATA
Rébuffat, Gaston.
[Etoiles et tempêres. English]
Starlight and storm/Gaston Rébuffat.
p. cm.
ISBN-13: 978-0-375-75506-4
1. Mountaineering—Alps. 2. Alps—Description and travel.
I. Title.
GV199.44.A4R42 1999
796.52'2'092—dc21 99-41400

Modern Library website address: www.modernlibrary.com

Printed in the United States of America

4 6 8 9 7 5

GASTON RÉBUFFAT

Gaston Rébuffat, mountaineer, writer, photographer, and filmmaker, was born in Marseilles on May 7, 1921. He spent his boyhood in Provence, where he first scaled the Calanques, the limestone pinnacles towering above the Mediterranean near Marseilles. At the age of twenty-one he earned certification as a professional mountain guide and subsequently became an instructor at the Ecole d'Alpinisme and the Ecole Militaire de Haute Montagne at Chamonix. Rébuffat gained international recognition in 1950 as a member of Maurice Herzog's triumphant French expedition that conquered the twenty-six-thousand-foot Annapurna peak in the

Himalayas. He was particularly noted for his numerous perilous ascents of Mont Blanc in the Alps.

Rébuffat's first book, *Etoiles et Tempêtes,* appeared in 1954. Subsequently published in English as *Starlight and Storm* (1956), it chronicles the ascent of six great north faces of the Alps. "Rébuffat's writing—easy and graceful as his movement up rock—is good enough to persuade us that a real enjoyment can be won from situations which to the rest of us would be hell," said the *New Statesman & Nation.* Sir John Hunt, one of the author's translators, noted: "Gaston Rébuffat, one of the great climbers of all time, is first and foremost an intensely human person, who has discovered through the medium of mountains the true perspective of living." A film version of *Etoiles et Tempêtes* was awarded the Grand Prix at the International Mountain and Exploration Film Festival at Trento, Italy, in 1958.

Rébuffat's next work, *Du Mont-Blanc à l'Himalaya* (1955; translated as *Mont Blanc to Everest* in 1956), is a superbly illustrated guide that surveys the sport of mountaineering from its beginnings to the conquest of Everest. "Many of the photographs are exquisite in themselves and brilliantly reproduced," said the *Man-*

chester Guardian. "The book makes its effect perhaps rather more like that of a work of music than of literature." *The New Yorker* agreed: "The photographs, which include views of the Rockies and of Alaskan mountains, notably Mount McKinley, are truly distinguished, and the ones in color are probably some of the most beautiful ever reproduced."

Neige et Roc (1959; translated as *On Snow and Rock* in 1963), Rébuffat's third book, presents instruction in the various techniques of mountain climbing. *Newsweek* called it "stirring and frightening" and said its brilliant photographs "can scarcely help but put the reader in Gaston Rébuffat's position—which is very often part way up some sheer wall of rock or snow or ice which seems impossible to climb and rises above an abyss."

In 1961 Rébuffat brought out the film *Entre Terre et Ciel,* a documentary chronicling two years of climbing in the French and Swiss Alps. Awarded the Grand Prix at the Tenth International Mountain and Exploration Film Festival at Trento, the movie inspired the lavishly illustrated book *Entre Terre et Ciel* (1962), which appeared in English as *Between Heaven and Earth* (1965). In *Cervin, Cime Exemplaire* (1965; translated as *Men and the Matter-*

horn in 1967) Rébuffat shares his own experiences ascending the Matterhorn, interlacing them with excerpts from the diaries of other famous climbers. "Rébuffat, noted guide and world lecturer [is] as agile with words as he is skilled," said *Library Journal.* "It is with love that he has compiled this history and embellished it with photographs of the Matterhorn in all its moods and seasons.... [His] ability to communicate a sensory excitement of nerve, spirit, and muscle is unique."

In 1969 Rébuffat published *Glace, Neige et Roc* (translated as *On Ice, Rock and Snow* in 1971), an updated edition of his earlier work *Neige et Roc.* "Rébuffat, already a legend among mountain climbers, is also a gifted writer who can translate the joys of scaling tall peaks into terms that have meaning to those who prefer to keep on the level," said the *Virginia Quarterly Review.* "This is an important book that will be classic in the literature of mountains and mountain climbing." In *Le Massif du Mont Blanc: Les 100 Plus Belles Courses* (1973; translated as *The Mont Blanc Massif: The 100 Fine Routes* in 1975) Rébuffat assists both experienced and novice climbers in choosing the finest and most elegant routes for tackling the Mont Blanc regions of the Alps. "The feel of the mountains and the upward imperative of the climber rise from this book like a delicate but compelling perfume," said the *Christian Science Monitor.* "Perhaps it is the breathtaking color photos of an expanse of assailable snow or the jagged teeth of a ridge reflecting a golden dawn. Perhaps it is the lyrical writing of Gaston Rébuffat."

A recipient of the Chevalier de la Légion d'honneur, Gaston Rébuffat died of cancer in Paris on May 31, 1985. "Gaston Rébuffat was a gifted author," eulogized Sir John Hunt in the *Times* (London). "His writing reflected the man. It was simple and sincere, seeking no sensational effects; almost, it could be described as poetic prose." Rébuffat's several books not published in English include *Mont-Blanc: Jardin Féerique* (1962); *Un Guide Raconte* (1964); *A la Rencontre du soleil* (1971); and *Les Horizons Gagnés* (1975).

Introduction to the Modern Library Exploration Series

Jon Krakauer

Why should we be interested in the jottings of explorers and adventurers? This question was first posed to me twenty-four years ago by a skeptical dean of Hampshire College upon receipt of my proposal for a senior thesis with the dubious title "Tombstones and the Moose's Tooth: Two Expeditions and Some Meandering Thoughts on Climbing Mountains." I couldn't really blame the guardians of the school's academic standards for thinking I was trying to bamboozle them, but in fact I wasn't. Hoping to convince Dean Turlington of my scholarly intent, I brandished an excerpt from *The Adventurer,* by Paul Zweig:

The oldest, most widespread stories in the world are adventure stories, about human heroes who venture into the myth-countries at the risk of their lives, and bring back tales of the world beyond men.... It could be argued... that the narrative art itself arose from the need to tell an adventure; that man risking his life in perilous encounters constitutes the original definition of what is worth talking about.

Zweig's eloquence carried the day, bumping me one step closer to a diploma. His words also do much to explain the profusion of titles about harrowing outdoor pursuits in bookstores these days. But even as the literature of adventure has lately enjoyed something of a popular revival, several classics of the genre have inexplicably remained out of print. The new Modern Library Exploration series is intended to rectify some of these oversights.

The four books we have selected to launch the series span four centuries of adventuring, providing a look at the shifting rationales given by explorers over the ages in response to the inevitable question: Why on earth would anyone willingly subject himself to such unthinkable hazards and hardships?

La Salle and the Discovery of the Great West, by the incomparable prose stylist Francis Parkman, recounts the astonishing journeys of Robert Cavelier, Sieur de La Salle, as he crisscrossed the wilds of seventeenth-century America in hopes of discovering a navigable waterway to the orient. La Salle did it, ostensibly at least, to claim new lands for King Louis XIV and to get rich. He succeeded on both counts—his explorations of the Mississippi Basin delivered the vast Louisiana Territory into the control of the French crown—but at no small personal cost: In 1687, after spending twenty of his forty-three years in the hostile wilderness of the New World, La Salle was shot in the head by mutinous members of his own party, stripped naked, and left in the woods to be eaten by scavenging animals.

Farthest North is a first-person narrative by the visionary Norse explorer Fridtjof Nansen, who in 1893 set sail from Norway with a crew of twelve in a wooden ship christened the *Fram*, hoping to discover the North Pole. Nansen's brilliant plan, derided as crazy by most of his peers, was to allow the *Fram* to become frozen into the treacherous pack ice of the Arctic Ocean, and then let prevailing currents carry the icebound ship north across the pole. Two years into the expedition, alas, and still more than 400 miles from his objective, Nansen realized that the drifting ice was not going to take the *Fram* all the way to the pole. Unfazed, he departed from the ship with a single companion and provisions for 100 days, determined to cover the remainder of the distance by dogsled, with no prospect of reuniting with the *Fram* for the return journey. The going was slow, perilous, and exhausting, but they got to within 261 statute miles of the pole before giving up and beginning a desperate, yearlong trudge back to civilization.

Unlike La Salle, Nansen couldn't plausibly defend his passion for exploration by claiming to do it for utilitarian ends. The North Pole was an exceedingly recondite goal, a geographical abstraction surrounded by an expanse of frozen sea that was of no apparent use to anybody. Nansen most often proffered what had by then become the justification de rigueur for jaunts to the ends of the earth—almighty science—but it didn't really wash.

Robert Falcon Scott, Nansen's contemporary, also relied on scientific rationale to justify his risky exploits, and it rang just as hollow. *The Last Place on Earth,* by English historian Roland Huntford, is the definitive, utterly riveting account of the race for the South Pole, which Scott lost to Nansen's protégé, Roald Amundsen, in 1911—and which cost Scott his life, as well. In death, Scott was mythologized as the preeminent tragic hero in the history of the British Empire, but Huntford's book—lauded by *The New York Times* as "one of the great debunking biographies"—portrays him as an inept bungler unworthy of such deification. Huntford also reveals that while Scott was marching toward his demise in Antarctica, his wife, Kathleen, was consummating an affair with his rival's mentor, Nansen, in a Berlin hotel room.

In the final title of the series, *Starlight and Storm,* the dashing French mountaineer Gaston Rébuffat recalls his ascents of the six great north faces of the Alps, including the notorious Eiger Nordwand, during the years following World War II. An incorrigible romantic, he describes his climbs in luminous, mesmerizing prose that is likely to inspire even dedicated flatlanders to pick up an ice-axe and light out for the great ranges. And how does Rébuffat reconcile the sport's matchless pleasures with its potentially lethal consequences? He resorts to bald-faced denial: "The real mountaineer," he insists, "does not like taking risks," and shuns danger like the plague. Although he acknowledges that in certain unavoidable situations "a thrill runs through him," he quickly (and unconvincingly) avows that it is "much too unpleasant a thrill for him to seek it out or to enjoy it."

If none of the extraordinary people featured in these chronicles adequately answers the nagging question—Why?—perhaps it is simply because adventurers, on the whole, are congenitally averse to leading examined lives. "If you have to ask," they like to mumble by way of dodging their inquisitors, "you just wouldn't understand." Rest assured, however, that the convolutions of the adventurous psyche are richly illuminated in these four compelling volumes, however enigmatic the protagonists may have remained to themselves.

INTRODUCTION

David Roberts

During the late 1940s and early 1950s, Gaston Rébuffat was one of the half-dozen best mountain climbers in the world. He could count among his peers only such men as the visionary Italian soloist Walter Bonatti; the fanatically driven Austrian Hermann Buhl (with whom, after a chance meeting on the Eiger, he would spearhead the grim survival epic chronicled in this book); and his fellow Chamonix guides, the powerhouse Lionel Terray and the mercurial acrobat Louis Lachenal. (At the time, no American or British climber was even in Rébuffat's league.)

On Annapurna in 1950, Rébuffat and Terray, forgoing any summit hopes of their own, saved the lives of

Lachenal and Maurice Herzog after that pair had staggered down from the top in a storm, exhausted and frostbitten. The triumph—the first ascent of any eight-thousand-meter peak—took a terrible toll, as Lachenal lost all his toes; Herzog, all his fingers and toes.

In 1954, as the thirty-two-year-old Rébuffat set out to write the book that would become *Starlight and Storm,* he was still bound by a contract the team had signed at the airport on their departure for Nepal. Sprung on the unsuspecting members, that contract forbade them to publish anything about the expedition for five years after its completion. The only account of the grand French adventure in the Himalayas would be that of its leader, Herzog. *Annapurna,* the now-canonic tale of perseverance, self-sacrifice, and heroism, would become the best-selling mountaineering book of all time.

By 1950, however, Rébuffat had serious ambitions to be a writer. He had already published a manual for beginning climbers and a photo book about the Calanques, the sea cliffs of his boyhood. As he read the interdicting contract, he was so shocked and dismayed that he came close to walking out of the airport and abandoning the expedition. At last he signed, but for the rest of his life, he nursed a bitter grievance about Herzog's preemptive strike.

It is in part for this reason that *Starlight and Storm* mentions Annapurna in only six glancing sentences. Forbidden to write about the expedition, Rébuffat turned to the climbs on which, in the long run, his lasting reputation would rest. During the 1930s, six great walls scattered across the Alps, all facing north, gained the cachet of ultimate challenges. They ranged from the appallingly steep, such as the Cima Grande di Lavaredo in the Italian Dolomites (overhanging in its first 720 feet, vertical thereafter), to the appallingly dangerous, such as the Eiger in Switzerland, where eight of the first ten men to attempt the face met their deaths.

By the time Rébuffat became a first-rate climber, in the early 1940s, all six faces had been climbed, but none had seen more than a handful of ascents. The winning of these precipices had made legends of their pioneers: the redoubtable Italian Ricardo Cassin (the only man to lead the first ascents of two of the six faces); the German Andreas Heckmair, "motor" of the extraordinary Eiger climb; and Pierre Allain, the greatest French alpinist of his day.

What was left for Rébuffat's generation, now that
these ultimate walls had succumbed? Without making
any particular fuss—today, his counterpart would no
doubt come decked out with commercial sponsorships
and hovered over by a media horde—Rébuffat set himself the goal of climbing all six of the great north faces
of the Alps. When he reached the top of the Eiger, on
July 29, 1952, Rébuffat accomplished this stirring feat of
virtuosity. It is a measure of the man's modesty that
nowhere in *Starlight and Storm* does he bother to mention
that he was the first man ever to seize the laurels from all
six of those perilous walls.

Confident though he was as a climber, at thirty-two
Rébuffat was by no means sure he had what it took to be
a "real" writer. Though he had grown up in Marseilles,
he had been obsessed with mountains since boyhood. So
brilliant were the alpine campaigns of his youth that in
1942 he was elected to the company of guides of Chamonix—an almost unheard-of honor for a climber not
born in Chamonix. (Terray, from Grenoble, and
Lachenal, of Annecy, were two other notable excep-
tions.) For two decades, the tall, craggy *montagnard* made
his living as a guide. To supplement their meager earn-

ings, Rébuffat and Terray conducted a ludicrous experiment in running a farm in Les Houches, just down the valley from Chamonix. (Since childhood, Gaston had had a mortal fear of cows. With both proprietors always off in the mountains, the farm did not last long.) *Starlight and Storm* is an odd crossbreed of a book. One wonders whether Arthaud, the original publisher, asked Rébuffat to beef up what they might have regarded as a dangerously slender account of six adventures in the mountains with a capsule how-to manual to give the work utilitarian value and shelf life.

Uncertain though he was in taking up the pen, the Chamonix guide found his voice at once, for he knew what he wanted to say about climbing and the mountain life. It is here that Rébuffat's utter originality comes to the fore. Ever since mountaineering had been "invented," with the first ascent of Mont Blanc in 1786, the struggle of men against the heights had been conceived of and narrated in martial terms. A team "laid siege" to a mountain; it "attacked" its objective by the likely "weaknesses" in its "defenses"; reaching the summit was inevitably a "victory," even a "conquest."

All this chest thumping was anathema to Rébuffat.

From an early age, he had gained his remarkable proficiency on slab and serac not by battling against the natural world but by embracing it. The mountain was not an enemy; it was an enchanted realm of peace and harmony, entered into in a spirit of communion, not of war.

In the lyrical hymn to that communion which poured out in the pages of *Starlight and Storm*, Rébuffat single-handedly revolutionized mountain writing. So thoroughly did this new aesthetic win the day, imbuing the next generation of climber-writers, that today's reader, picking up *Starlight and Storm* for the first time, can scarcely sense how radical this sort of writing seemed in 1954.

Indeed, at times Rébuffat's exaltations threaten to eclipse the real tragedies and do-or-die struggles he endured. One must read between the lines to sense the horror of his party's bivouac on the descent of the Grandes Jorasses after Rébuffat's companion Georges Michel has been swept 1,500 feet to his death by a falling boulder—not to mention the astounding skill by which Rébuffat himself avoided the same death by instinctively jamming his plunging body into a perfect chimney position thirty feet below the ledge, at the cost of a broken foot, kneecap, and rib.

After 1953, Rébuffat continued to guide, often taking clients up lines otherwise considered too stiff for amateurs. But he receded from the cutting edge of first ascents and new routes. Instead, in collaboration with several gifted photographers, he produced a series of exquisite picture books that mingled personal reflection with historical evocation of the alpine playground. These books—*Neige et Roc, Entre Terre et Ciel, Mont-Blanc: Jardin Féerique,* and others—gained a large audience and made Rébuffat mildly famous.

In the photos illustrating those books, Rébuffat appeared again and again in profile against a vertical cliff, always wearing the same patterned pullover sweater, the rope dangling from his waist into the void, hands seeming to caress the rock, toes perched on invisible holds. These images captured as none had before the grace and elegance that lay at the heart of Rébuffat's approach to climbing.

So persuasive was the Rébuffat aesthetic that it inspired a counterreaction among the blue-collar Brits who began to make their own mark on mountaineering in the 1960s. "Ghastly Rubberfat," they wickedly nicknamed their French rival, and their quarrel with Rébuffat's cult of grace and technique found voice in a delightful essay, called "Apes or Ballerinas?" by the Scottish ice climber and satirist Tom Patey. Patey argued, only partly tongue in cheek, that getting up a climb depended on the thrashing primate emerging from beneath the veneer of the stylish gymnast that Rébuffat so photogenically personified.

—

One day in 1959, in a bookstore in Boulder, I held in my hands a small volume, recently published by E. P. Dutton & Co., called *Starlight and Storm*. At sixteen, starting to fall under the spell of the Colorado mountains, I had read *Annapurna* and learned of Rébuffat's key role in that bold and costly ascent. But of these six great north faces in the Alps, I knew nothing. The photos spoke to me of some world of mountain exploit far more daunting than what could be found on the talus piles of my beloved Rockies. I hesitated in the face of the book's $5.50 price tag. For that much money, I could buy three karabiners!

Along with *Annapurna* and Lionel Terray's *Conquistadors of the Useless* (published in English a few years later),

Starlight and Storm became for me a sacred text. It was these three books, as much as the outings I performed with my chums, that turned me from a hiker into a serious mountaineer. Still without any inkling that I might ever climb a big wall myself, I thrilled through each rereading of the harrowing bivouacs, the gutsy leads up frozen pitches, that Rébuffat so poetically recounted.

At the age of twenty, by now a junior instructor at Colorado Outward Bound School, I was asked to give a dawn inspirational reading to the mob of ninety-six students it was our job to toughen up in the Elk Range. With trembling voice but the passion of an acolyte, I read the passage in *Starlight and Storm* called "The Brotherhood of the Rope."

Rereading Rébuffat's prose more than three decades later, I am struck anew by the originality of his writing. Perhaps in 1959 it was the how-to treatise called "The Beginning Climber" that made me dig deep into my pockets and buy *Starlight and Storm*, for I was still too green to know that you couldn't learn to climb from a book.

In reprinting Rébuffat in 1999, one is tempted to omit these now thoroughly outdated instructional pages, which Rébuffat adjoined so chimerically to his six splendid stories. Yet I find the very obsolescence of his advice beguiling. To think, that as late as 1954, echoing the wisdom of his day, Rébuffat still recommended the frequent use of the shoulder stand and the Tyrolean traverse or, in teaching the rappel, told us to "double the rope and hang it over a projecting rock"!

What is more, sprinkled through the blunt and pragmatic injunctions of "The Beginning Climber" are all kinds of philosophical nuggets (to Rébuffat, climbing could never be reduced to mere rules). "Reading a map is a thrilling pastime," he insists. "Of course, technique is a poor thing, even a wretched thing, when separated from the heart which has guided it: this is true in rock climbing, or playing a piano, or building a cathedral."

Over the years, I am sorry to say, I had begun to take Rébuffat for granted. His Saint-Exupéry approach to mountaineering was only one vein. In the late 1960s, caught up in the raucous, antiestablishment antics of my own gang of climbing cronies, I sympathized with Tom Patey's witty put-down of Rébuffat rather than with the mystic enthusiasms that had so inspired me at sixteen.

During the last two years, however, as I have conducted research for a book about what really happened on Annapurna in 1950, I have discovered a new and far more complex Gaston Rébuffat than the one that had been lodged in my head. With the posthumous publication of his letters to his wife, Françoise, in 1996, the full measure of Rébuffat's disenchantment on Annapurna came to light. Above all, he was disgusted from the start with the fog of French chauvinism that surrounded the expedition—to which Herzog would unblushingly appeal in *Annapurna*. Louis Lachenal, equally disenchanted, was likewise silenced by the contract he had signed interdicting publication for five years.

Both men had been mortified by a ceremony in Paris prior to departure during which the team members were commanded to swear an oath of unquestioning obedience to Herzog. At that meeting, Lucien Devies, the most powerful man in French mountaineering and a Gaullist as staunch as Herzog, delivered a pep talk invoking French glory and military efficiency. Under his breath, afterward, Lachenal muttered, "On our knees we will go," and Rébuffat, picking up the sardonic thread, echoed, "With joy in our hearts!" In his notebook, Rébuffat characterized the session: "Depersonalization... a certain Nazification."

Through the rest of his life, Rébuffat longed to publish his own commentary on Annapurna; but Françoise, conscious of the fact that the 1950 ascent had woven itself so deeply into France's myth of itself that her husband's views might be greeted as the darkest apostasy, counseled him to keep his silence. When Herzog, in the early 1980s, published an even more self-serving version of the climb in a book called *Les Grandes Aventures de l'Himalaya*, Rébuffat scribbled his bitter rejoinders in the margins of his copy, and made further notes toward the commentary he would never publish.

Yet when these glimmerings surfaced in the last few years, more than a decade after Rébuffat's death, far from revealing the guide as a traitor to the sacred myth of Annapurna, they were widely hailed as a long overdue debunking of that myth, stated with terse eloquence. Rébuffat saw Herzog, even on the summit, as consciously orchestrating the heroic role he would play the rest of his life. There, atop the highest mountain yet climbed in the world, Herzog had insisted on Lachenal's photographing himself holding aloft the French tricolor, the flag of the French Alpine Club, and even the flag of the tire company for which he worked, Kléber Colombes.

Yet moments later he foolishly dropped his gloves, which rolled into the void—an error that would cost Herzog his fingers.

"Ah, if only Herzog had lost his flags instead of his gloves, how happy I would have been!" wrote Rébuffat in his private notes. And, conjuring up the summit moment: "After the sequence of the flags, this jingoistic and supremely pragmatic moment, Maurice organized his ecstasy. Losing, if not his reason, at least his sense of reality, he began complacently to soar, plunged into a kind of happiness, a beatitude of the moment when a sense of the real ought to have been primordial." Only the cannier Lachenal sensed the absolute need to get down at once, and it can be argued that he lost his toes because he refused to abandon Herzog, whose tranced-out obliviousness would almost certainly otherwise have meant his death.

To read only the Rébuffat of his published works is to imagine a gentle poet of the mountains, a philosopher of harmony and rapture. The other Rébuffat, who has emerged in the posthumous letters and notes—the unblinking critic of all that was hypocritical, nationalistic, and egomaniacal in mountaineering—was there all along. His closest friends knew this; they knew, for example, how on the Eiger, Rébuffat was driven to a fury by Hermann Buhl's pigheaded refusal to share the lead, even when Buhl's lapses of judgment might have cost the lives of any number of the nine climbers trapped together in their desperate fight for the summit.

Last April I met Françoise in Paris, where she lives. Though remarried, she fiercely guards her first husband's legacy. Rébuffat was diagnosed with breast cancer in 1975. In the decade it took him to die, he spiraled downward in an agonizing sequence of small losses and setbacks. Though mortally stricken, Gaston made one last hard climb, on the Aiguille du Midi in 1983.

Two years before he died, fulfilling a lifelong dream, Rébuffat rafted the Colorado River with Françoise, signing up for a commercial trip. "He was very tired, just out of chemotherapy," she told me. "There were clients of all ages on the river. They quickly saw that Gaston was very sick. Very discreetly, the other clients started to do everything for him. To get in and out of the boat, he needed help. Two young Germans found the best campsites for him."

Did these companions realize who Rébuffat was? I

questioned. Did they know what this man had done in the mountains in his prime?

"No," said Françoise. "All they knew was that he was French and that he was very sick."

In light of all I have learned about Annapurna in the last two years and having talked to his widow and his surviving friends, I have gained a new admiration for Gaston Rébuffat. He becomes in my eyes a very different man from the lyric climber who enthralled me at sixteen. Yet he emerges, I think, as a hero of even greater stature than the first man to climb the six great north faces—a hero for the twenty-first century, not the mid-twentieth.

In this timely republication of *Starlight and Storm*, a whole new generation of readers has the happy chance to discover a blithe, ageless book that stands as one of the finest testaments to the exploratory spirit ever written.

———

David Roberts writes often about mountain climbing, exploration, and archaeology. His book about what happened on Annapurna in 1950 will be published by Simon & Schuster next year.

CONTENTS

FOREWORD

Any man who has achieved the record of daring, endurance, and skill recounted in this book must be, in the nature of things, a very remarkable person. No one who reads this story can fail to be fascinated, not only by the adventures in the vertical but by the manner of their telling and by the character of the man who performed them. What kind of a man is Gaston Rébuffat?

I count myself fortunate to be his friend, although our acquaintance goes back only as far as 1951. Already by then, at the age of thirty, touched by fame for his exploits in the Alps and recognized as one of the foremost Alpine guides, he had just returned from a Himalayan expedition which had attracted world attention—the French ascent of Annapurna, the highest mountain climbed at that time; a blaze of glory enveloped Maurice Herzog and his men. My wife and I had planned to celebrate an anniversary by climbing with Gaston one of the great classic rock routes on the Chamonix Aiguilles, and Gaston met us at the station, pushing a bicycle. Together we walked beside the River Arve towards his rooms in a chalet near the village of Les Praz, and as we walked and discussed our plans and other topics, I was able to study the man.

His appearance and bearing gave an immediate impression of alertness, purpose and dynamic energy. A small but striking head, habitually backtilted. Narrow features, lantern-jawed, with forward-thrusting chin. An unruffled brow, rather low, topped by a remarkable dense bush of upstanding black hair. Brown eyes, deep set beneath jutting brows, intent, direct and searching, quickly lit by humour. His frame long and lean, with high, strong shoulders, he walked with a loose, loping, almost bouncing gait. He spoke with slow emphasis, his voice soft, drawling, and with the slightly nasal twang of Southern France. I noticed the neatness, indeed the gaiety of his clothes: the bright checked shirt, the black-and-white patterned jersey, the pale grey cloth breeches and white cabled stockings, covering long slim legs, thrust into his loose-fitting mountain boots.

He made us feel at ease from the start: there was a complete absence of arrogance and shyness alike. He spoke of Annapurna—not of the difficulties and the hardships, although these had not been lacking, for Gaston himself had been one of the four to return, frost-bitten and snow-blinded, from the highest camp: but of the human problems of that great drama, of our mutual friends among the Sherpas, of the beauties of the foot-hills. He talked of our plans for the next two days—modest enough for him—with the exuberance of a schoolboy on the eve of his first Alpine climb. Later, in his rooms, sitting with his charming wife Françoise and their small daughter Frédérique, he showed me photographs of some of his outstanding exploits at that time: the Matterhorn north face and the north-east face of Badile were among them. Since then, he has, of course, added many new routes of extreme difficulty to the history of Alpine mountaineering.

I noticed that his interest in these achievements lay

more in his companions, the circumstances and atmosphere of the climbs, than in the technical problems they afforded. Here was a man in love with his mountains, an ace performer unconscious of his virtuosity. We found ourselves at once in sympathy, and friendship grew quickly.

That night snow fell heavily and next morning, with the clouds hanging low and the rocks plastered thickly, we had to abandon our cherished plan. After wading day-long and thigh-deep up to the Grands Mulets hut, we even gave up a futile struggle to ascend Mont Blanc, and spent the following day scaling the slippery rock needles of Clocher-Clochetons in a drizzle. But the disappointment was lessened by the company of our new friend. We found him not only a good talker but a keen listener; and he talked well of men and mountains.

Since that day I have had several other occasions among the mountains with Gaston: all have been singularly ill-fated from the weather point of view: indeed the only successful climbs done together have been on those rock needles above the meadows of Plan-Praz and on the boulders in the Forest of Fontainebleau. And there have been many other meetings, far from the mountain scene. But whether it be among the hills or on a Paris boulevard, whether in a mountain hut or in his chalet above Chamonix, Gaston is just the same. Always he speaks of the mountains, his reminiscences of adventures shared among them with friends, and his plans for fresh adventures with clients—and his clients are also his friends.

It was natural that I should invite Gaston to act as agent for the equipment we needed from French firms for the Everest Expedition, and this task he carried out with a devotion and enthusiasm typical of the man; his excitement over our triumph made me feel glad that he should have had a share in the story of Everest.

Gaston Rébuffat, one of the great climbers of all time, is first and foremost an intensely human person, who has discovered through the medium of mountains the true perspective of living.

JOHN HUNT

INTRODUCTORY

This book is the record of a young man's life devoted entirely to high mountains. For years, while I lived in Marseilles, I dreamed of climbing mountains. Each winter I found myself impatiently awaiting July. At last the day would come for departure to Ailefroide or Chamonix. There I would spend a few days on the tops, only to return and wait for another year. Then one day, deciding that I must live among mountains, I became a guide.

Two climbs especially gave expression to these dreams of my youth: the Barre des Ecrins, climbed while I was a boy, and the north face of the Grandes Jorasses by the Walker Spur, which I climbed in my early twenties. Coming down from the Jorasses in 1945, I found I had rid myself of my amateur ambitions, and my desire for high places assumed a new quality. I left the National Ski and Mountaineering School at which I was an instructor and took up my profession as guide. It seemed to me that I was now complete master of my destiny.

A dream which comes true leads to other dreams. After the Walker Spur of the Grandes Jorasses I wanted to climb the other north faces, the Drus, Badile, Matterhorn, Cima Grande and Eiger. When these faces were untrodden I was still a child; now that I was of an age to climb them, I wanted to climb them all. But that by itself would not have been enough. I was a guide; I wanted to climb them as a guide, in the course of my duties, for youth is exacting and uncompromising. On the Ecrins I had the Boy Scout outlook. On the Grandes Jorasses and during the four years that I spent at the headquarters of the "Jeunesse et Montagne" school, the Military School of Mountain Training and the National Ski and Mountaineering School, I was still an exuberant boy. The profession of guide helped me to become a man; it is among the finest that exist, for it is practised in the unspoilt regions of the earth's surface.

In this modern age, very little remains that is real. Night has been banished, so have the cold, the wind and the stars. They have all been neutralized: the rhythm of life itself is obscured. Everything goes so fast and makes so much noise, and men hurry by without heeding the grass by the roadside, its colour, its smell and the way it shimmers when the wind caresses it. What a strange encounter then is that between man and the high places of his planet! Up there he is surrounded by the silence of forgetfulness. If there is a slope of snow steep as a glass window, he climbs it, leaving behind him a strange trail. If there is a rock perfect as an obelisk, he defies gravity and proves that he can get up anywhere.

Guides are no foolhardy adventurers: they live, they do their job. Every day in the summer they get up very early to question the sky and the wind. The day before, perhaps, they were uneasy, for long clouds scarred the western horizon. They feared a night of worsening weather; the Milky Way shone too brightly, the cold delayed its coming. But now, if the north wind has won the upper hand, the weather is good, the guide can rouse his client and set out. Then the rope will join together two beings who now live as one. During these hours the guide is linked with a stranger who will become a friend. When two men share the good and the bad, then they are no longer strangers.

This profession might become wearisome through the repetition of the same climbs time after time, but the guide is more than a mere machine for climbing rocks and ice slopes, for knowing the weather and the way. He does not climb for himself, he throws open the gates of his mountains as a gardener opens the gates of his garden. The heights are a splendid setting for his work, and climbing gives him a pleasure of which he never tires. But above all he is repaid by the pleasure of the man he guides. He knows that such-and-such a climb is particularly interesting, that at this turn the view is quite suddenly very beautiful, and that this ice ridge is delicate as lace. He says nothing of all this, but his reward is in his companion's smile of discovery. If the guide thought to win his pleasure only from his own climbing, he would be robbed of it and soon tire of the mountains. In fact, though he may climb the same crack or the same slope five, ten or twenty times a summer, he rejoices each time to renew acquaintance. But his real happiness derives from a deeper pleasure, that of his kinship with the mountains and the elements, just as the peasant is akin to the soil or the workman to the materials with which he works. If the second man on the rope hesitates, the guide restores his confidence. If the storm breaks suddenly, he knows its secrets, his instinct masters it, his sense of responsibility multiplies his strength tenfold and he brings his party back safe to the hut. He loves difficulty but abhors danger, which is a very different thing. Sometimes, it is true, he is killed by lightning, stone-fall, or avalanche. That too is part of the job; but so long as he lives he strives to lead his rope safely.

Very often the natives of Chamonix or the other mountain valleys are guides from father to son. I come from Marseilles, and it was in my native Provence, on the hills of the Sainte Baume and the Luberon, and on the sea cliffs of the Calanques[1], that I learned to love wind and wide spaces, starlight and storm, flowers and forests, the taste and smell of all these.

In 1950 I was with the French expedition to the Hi-

---

[1] A line of limestone cliffs near Marseilles: a well-known training ground of rock-climbers.

malaya. On Annapurna¹, as on the Ecrins or the Jorasses, we were guided by the same dream. At first we felt a pleasing sense of awe, face to face with these gigantic peaks; then we entered into their secret places. We walked, we explored, we climbed, and every evening we slept the sleep of happiness under the sky of Asia. Wood fires, camps in the valleys, camps on the glaciers in the Himalaya, evenings and sunsets in Alpine huts—these nights in the mountains are among the fairest memories of a climber's life. But the most lasting and often the best are the bivouacs on the earth itself, under the stars.

To succeed in scaling the great north faces, the pioneers had to climb for two or three days and spend at least one night clinging to the face. Nowadays, despite our knowledge of the routes, you still very often have to bivouac on some of them. But this is no drawback. At the end of the day the mountaineer looks for a ledge, lays down his sack, hammers in a piton and attaches himself to it. After the hard, acrobatic effort of the climb he is lost—like the poet—in contemplation; but to a greater

¹ 26,493 feet. The summit was reached on 3rd June. The descent involved a night in a crevasse and severe frost-bite. See Maurice Herzog, *Annapurna* (Jonathan Cape Ltd. 1952).

degree than the poet he can be a part of the hills around. The man who bivouacs becomes one with the mountain. On his bed of stone, leaning against the great wall, facing empty space which has become his friend, he watches the sun fade over the horizon on his left, while on his right the sky spreads its mantle of stars. At first he is wakeful, then, if he can, he sleeps; then wakes again, watches the stars and sleeps again; then at last he stays awake and watches. On his right the sun will return, having made its great voyage below this shield of scattered diamonds.

The man who climbs only in good weather, starting from huts and never bivouacking, appreciates the splendour of the mountains but not their mystery, the dark of their night, the depth of their sky above. I know enthusiastic lads who flee the city at week-ends to the Forest of Fontainebleau or the Calanques. On the Sunday they climb, but beforehand, on the Saturday evening, they bivouac. Theirs is the taste for nature and the universe. On the other hand, some mountaineers are proud of having done all their climbs without bivouac. How much they have missed! And the same applies to those who *only* enjoy rock-climbing, or only the ice climbs, only the ridges or the faces. We should refuse none of the thousand and one joys that the mountains offer us at every turn. We should brush nothing aside, set no restrictions. We should experience hunger and thirst, be able to go fast, but also know how to go slowly and to contemplate. Variety is the spice of life.

There are some north faces on which, thanks to knowledge of the route and the pitons left by other parties, it is no longer necessary to bivouac, as it was when they were first climbed. The Cima Grande di Lavaredo is one of these. But climbing that face I thought more than once of the pioneers clinging the night through to the wall of vertical white stone soaring above their heads to the stars. Of course one *can* bivouac for the sake of bivouacking, just as one can climb for the sake of climbing, but that is not our calling. There is little satisfaction in being either a spectator or a robot. We must be one with the night, with the mountain; our role is not to stand aside.

The stars shine in the sky and the mountaineer can see them. They have a life of their own, yet in a sense they belong to his life, too; for on them depends his fate. If they shine he is happy; if they shine too brightly he is filled with doubt, for a storm is on the way. If the clouds have veiled them, snow will fall in the early morning.

Electricity may have banished them from man's life in the valley, but on high places their golden crystals are a part of his very being.

—

This evening, as I write these lines, the desire seizes me to breathe the night air for a few minutes. It is winter, and cold. Hemmed in between two black masses of houses, fringed by the roofs of my narrow street, the stars seem to be moving slowly as I advance.

"It's cold," I say to myself, "that's a good sign. The snow will be hard."

How stupid of me! Am I not in Paris, in the Rue des Grands-Augustins? But my street leads on to the quays where the Seine, with its sentinel trees, and the quiet night combine to recall nature, even in the heart of the great city. It is both early and late. It is the hour when mountaineers go out on to the hut terrace to scan the sky, test the wind and the snow. It is cold, and cold nights mean fine days. It is the time to light the lantern and start out....

Here in Paris I dream of high hills.

GASTON RÉBUFFAT
PARIS, 1953

STARLIGHT AND STORM

THE NORTH FACE OF THE GRANDES JORASSES

1. THE WALKER SPUR

The north face of the Grandes Jorasses is a difficult
climb; but besides that it is a thing of beauty. Nearly
4,000 feet high and nearly 5,000 feet wide, it resembles a
cathedral. Its top reaches 13,800 feet. The glacier flows
like a great ribbon at its base. Set amid a huge amphitheatre of ice, the face is not visible from the valley.
But it has a fascination of its own and many come up to
see it. The tourist on his way to the Couvercle hut sees
it coming into view as he climbs the Egralets; from the
Aiguille du Moine or the Aiguille Verte one gazes upon

its full immensity: a block of granite tawny and grey, as high as four Eiffel Towers one on top of the other. Solid yet shapely, it has grace despite its bulk. Its crest is half-way to heaven. It is a living thing. This is no worn stone that crumbles and collapses. It reaches skywards; but beneath the Leschaux glacier its roots push deep into the warm and living earth.

I have passed many an evening on the terrace of the Couvercle hut, looking up at it in the hour when the sun touches only the highest tops. Already it is night in the valleys and dusk clothes the lower mountains. Up there the fire is smouldering, glowing; then in a few moments the north face of the Grandes Jorasses is ablaze. Down below everything remains calm, gripped by the frost. The cold climbs up the great couloirs, the last rays slowly leave the wall and abandon it to night.

Then comes a dead time when life seems to hang suspended. The faint sounds are no more than murmurs. But after this interval another life begins: one by one the stars burst through the great vault, they gleam and twinkle in a countless brotherhood. Meanwhile it is very cold; everything around creaks and crackles. And like many other mountaineers I stand there on the hut terrace. I know the spectacle by heart, yet it draws me and stirs me again and again; and while men sleep and the earth rolls on in space, there appears to some, in their dreams, the vision of the great north face.

———

Like many other mountains, the Grandes Jorasses were first climbed by their sunny, welcoming south side. The summit ridge, about three-quarters of a mile long and over 13,000 feet high, comprises the following points: the Pointe Young (13,120 feet), the Pointe Margarita (13,337 feet), the Pointe Michel Croz (13,474 feet), the Pointe Whymper (13,767 feet), and the summit itself, the Pointe Walker, 13,800 feet high. Each name marks a stage in the hard-won conquest of this mountain. After the south face the climbers attacked the ridges: the Arête des Hirondelles—the ridge of the swallows—so pure in its downward sweep, was not climbed until 1927, by the Italians Matteoda, Ravelli, and Rivetti, led by the guides Adolphe Rey and Alphonse Chenoz.[1]

But the north face remained virgin despite numerous attacks upon it. The great wall became a grim challenge;

[1] It had been descended in 1911 by G. Winthrop Young, Josef Knubel, and H. O. Jones.

desire turned to fear, until it evoked real terror in men's hearts. Some of the finest mountaineers approached its base, both guided and guideless, British, German, Austrian, Italian, Swiss, French. And there were some who died there.

As early as 1907 Geoffrey Winthrop Young and Josef Knubel had made a reconnaissance; they were the first to feel the urge to climb the most magnificent north face of the Alps. But no serious attempts were made until 1928, up the spur of the Pointe Walker. Gasparotto, Rand Herron[1] and Zanetti, guided by Armand Charlet and Evariste Croux, reached the foot of the first barrier of slabs, at a height of about 10,800 feet. Then, after an interval of three years, further attempts were made in 1931, and continued in regular sequence until success was won. On 1st July 1931 two Germans, Heckmair and Kroner, made an attempt up the central couloir. A few days later two other Germans, Brehm and Rittler, started off by the same route. They fell and were killed, probably by an avalanche or stone-fall. Their bodies

[1] On the return from a Himalayan expedition to Nanga Parbat in 1932 Rand Herron, an American, was killed descending the Great Pyramid.

were found a week later by Heckmair and Kroner, who were making another attempt.

The north face of the Grandes Jorasses became the most coveted prize in the Alps; the best mountaineers of the day set off one after the other from the Leschaux hut, the starting-point for climbers in the Jorasses amphitheatre. There were the Germans: Franz Schmid, conqueror of the north face of the Matterhorn, Steinauer and Welzenbach[1]; the Italians, Binel and Cretier, Boccalatte and Chabod, Carrel and Maquignaz; the French, Dilleman and Couturier, guided by Armand Charlet. But not one of these parties succeeded in climbing the first rock barrier.

In 1933 another route was tried. Abandoning the Walker Spur the Italians, Gervasutti and Zanetti, reached 11,500 feet on the central spur, which leads to the Pointe Michel Croz. Gervasutti was one of the best climbers of all time, and a most endearing character[2]. A year later, on 5th July 1934, Armand Charlet and Robert Greloz reached 11,800 feet on the same spur, in an attempt which

[1] Later killed in 1934 on Nanga Parbat, 26,620 feet, in the Himalaya.
[2] He died on Mont Blanc du Tacul some years later.

caused quite a stir at the time. This attempt was closely followed by that of two Swiss, Loulou Boulaz, a girl of frail appearance but exceptional willpower, and Raymond Lambert[1], who attacked the face. Then it was the Germans again, Meier and Steinauer. Indeed on 30th July there were no less than four parties spread out over the spur: a very fast French party, Armand Charlet and Fernand Belin; an Italian party, Gervasutti and Chabod; an Austrian party, and finally a German party, Peters and Haringer.

In the face of bad conditions and uncertain weather all the parties gave up except Peters and Haringer. But after passing the first obstacle, a vertical rock step, they too were obliged to turn. During their dangerous descent, with fresh snow and ice on the rocks, Haringer slipped and fell to the glacier 1,700 feet below. Peters reached Chamonix alone, after spending five days and four nights on the face.

A lesser man than Peters would have accepted defeat. But the following year he was the first to lay siege to the wall, with Meier replacing Haringer. After an attempt held up by stone-falls the two Germans succeeded in

---

[1] In 1952 he climbed to 28,000 feet on Everest.

making their triumphal first ascent on 28th and 29th June 1935. A few days later the climb was repeated, first by Gervasutti and Chabod, then by Loulou Boulaz and Raymond Lambert, then by Messner and Steinauer.

A great step forward had been taken in the conquest of the north face of the Jorasses, but the real problem had not been solved. The Pointe Michel Croz (13,474 feet) is only one of the points on the summit ridge, whereas the summit itself is the Pointe Walker (13,800 feet), and the idea of an elegant direct route joining glacier to summit with no detours again filled the minds of mountaineers. The best French climber of the day, Pierre Allain, made a reconnaissance with Edward Frendo in 1937, followed the year after by an attempt with Jean Leininger. The Walker Spur was a climb well within the powers of Pierre. Indeed he was the first to overcome the barrier of rock slabs which had stopped every attempt so far. But with this obstacle behind him he gave up. The date was 1st August.

On the same day three Italian climbers, quite un-known in the Western Alps but with some great first as-cents behind them in the Dolomites, crossed the frontier at the Col du Géant, descended the French side of the

Mont Blanc range, stopped at the Requin hut and ingenuously asked the custodian:

"Can you please tell us where the north face of the Grandes Jorasses is?"

Surprised and amused by these joking Italians, the custodian pointed vaguely. "It's up there." Two nights later the custodian of the Couvercle hut thought he must be dreaming when he saw a tiny light on the Walker Spur, at 11,150 feet; and the next night he saw the same tiny light 1,300 feet higher, on the upper third of the face. The climbers passed the third night on the summit, in a storm. And so it came about that with no drums beating or flags flying the Italian climbers Cassin, Esposito and Tizzoni succeeded, thanks to their great confidence, resolution and modern technique, in making the first ascent of the direct route up the north face of the Grandes Jorasses, the most splendid climb in all the Alps.

During those August days of 1938 I had the good fortune to be making my first acquaintance with the high hills. I was seventeen, and too absorbed with my début on the Ecrins and Meije to have any other desires. But during the following summers, after doing some of the bigger climbs, then some of the exceptionally severe routes, my enthusiastic mind began to conceive the finest plan of all: to climb the north face of the Grandes Jorasses. It is a wonderful thing, and perhaps a necessary thing too, for a boy to have a plan in his head. Certainly the Pointe Walker is a great summit, and its ascent by the northern spur the hardest climb in the Alps, but such definitions are really no more than a form of words. For me this mountain was the mountain of my dreams, and this climb the supreme moment of my youth.

—

How strange it was, on the eve of great events, to be in the little Leschaux hut at the foot of the north face. Here I was at last, after desiring this moment so long, after such long preparations! Lying in the bunks, our eyes wide open in the darkness, we waited for the deliverance of morning. Just now my companion, Edward Frendo, had an air of unconcern, but I knew that he was anxious. He had already tried before. For myself, I had no experience of this side of the mountain at all; but I was uneasy in these final moments of waiting and I could not sleep.

To my troubled mind there came the memory of my first night in the mountains and my first climb, six years before. It makes an interesting comparison with this occasion. Then, it was a sort of baptism. Lying out in the open, eyes turned up to the stars, we were bivouacking on the Col des Avalanches. Next day we were going to do the Barre des Ecrins (13,462 feet), a dream of many years past. I was seventeen years old and rather frail. Despite the cold I fell asleep.

Now, to-day, I was no longer weak. I felt in my head, in my whole body, that strength which I then had needed so badly down in the valley. Soon it would go coursing through me, in the next few days, when we would be climbing all the time without a pause.

Down in the valley I have often been told that climbing is a useless pursuit. My answer is: "You can't understand." Sometimes I have been asked if my happiness is due to worldly wealth!

A little time ago I was still a child. I was carefree; yet deep within me I nursed a longing for some revelation. At the age of seventeen I was preparing to tackle the big mountains; I had already glimpsed them four years earlier, thanks to a boyish escapade. From Ailefroide, where

I was on holiday, I had followed three mountaineers covertly, at a distance, on their way to the Caron hut. That was how I first saw the Barre des Ecrins. For the first time in my life I was in the presence of a great mountain. That night I ran down to the valley, conjuring up fantastic deeds, as children do. I had to wait four years—and how impatiently I waited!

I had already climbed rocks, for all children play at climbing, but never "the real thing" on a mountain. "The real thing": it summed up my longing. This ridge of the Ecrins, over 13,000 feet high, was no longer just a mountain marked on a map, it lived in my boyish mind. I said nothing to my mother, for fear that she might oppose my plans. I was thought to be absent-minded; in reality I was burning with desire. I was at the age of sublime enthusiasms, the age when one grows too quickly out of clothes which are always too short.

At last, one day, I contrived to make the acquaintance of a real mountaineer: Henri Moulin. Under a bulky frame and behind a loud voice he concealed a very real kindness. If at the beginning my visits were not entirely disinterested—for had he not, among other climbs, done the Ecrins?—Moulin soon became my friend and elder brother. At last, in one of our many conversations, he said to me:

"We might do the Barre des Ecrins together next summer, and the Meije too perhaps."

I blushed all over with happiness. When I left his house I was utterly absorbed in my dream. Nothing else existed around me. At seventeen the Ecrins represented, for me, the one thing worth living for, and I read and reread everything that I could lay hands on about this awe-inspiring mountain. I did not dare to go back to Moulin for fear that he might have changed his mind. I lived through a springtime of alternating fear and joy at the prospect of summer to come. I made plans, but a moment later they seemed like castles in the air. So I focussed my ambitions on the project in hand, but the thought of a storm on the day of the climb, or of the snow failing to freeze, would be enough to put it out of reach. One evening I could stand it no longer; I ran to Moulin's house.

"Sit down. What's the matter?"

Everything was the matter. I was so anxious. Suppose the snow didn't freeze? Suppose the storm...? But Moulin, solid as oak, radiated confidence. He would *make* the snow freeze, he would put off the storm. I left him, reassured, then on the staircase I remembered that I had forgotten to ask him one question. I climbed up again, and had not passed the doorway before I burst out: "And the bergschrund. Shall we be able to get across that?"

He roared with laughter, making me feel ridiculously small. He pretended to reflect, then he said: "We'll cross it on the right. But you must make yourself light. Then above that..."

I went off, this time completely reassured.

July came, and we left for La Bérarde. Two days later we were bivouacking on the rocks of the Col des Avalanches. The night was hard and cold at 10,800 feet, but we had both preferred a bivouac on the mountain itself to the hut. In a vague way we felt that this was how it ought to be. And there, in front of us, was the south face of the Ecrins which we were to climb.

In the very early morning we walked in silence to the attack. We made no stir as we passed; the mountain seemed not to notice us at all, and I felt vaguely disappointed. I was so happy that I would have liked everything to share in my happiness, but up there on the rocks above us the sun lingered, ignoring our presence. Now we were at the rocks, and Moulin climbed the first slab. Then it was my turn. I struggled, panted, scraped the skin off my knees and fingers, but I did not linger long; at seventeen climbing is still an instinctive movement. I climbed cautiously, but with a gay heart. For the first time I tasted the serious thrill of a real climb. I was discovering my own body, which I had wrenched from the earth below and which was supported only by the grip of two fingers. It seemed to me that I had never really lived before this moment.

At a delicate step I was afraid, with that fear which shames and paralyses the faculties. There, down below, was empty space... But my companion above restored confidence. We went on. How many important events there are in a climb! Then, as now, I found little pleasure in the mere sense of overcoming danger; but rather, as familiarity with the consciousness of space around slowly grew on me, I felt in the right place on this ridge of grey rock, perched between heaven and earth. I look back at it even now with a sense of exaltation. I see again the hemp rope thread-like against the wall, binding together two

young men supremely conscious of their bodies, express-
ing thus the blossoming of life.

We stood for a long time on the summit, proud at
heart and gravely rejoicing in the unfolding of the world
around us, in the tiredness of our muscles, in the smiles
exchanged. That midday on the top of the Ecrins it
seemed to me that I was born a second time. In these few
hours I had made so many discoveries! Moulin pointed
out to me the summits around, pictures to dream of for
winters to come: the Pelvoux, the Ailefroide, the Meije;
behind, Mont Blanc and the Matterhorn; and far, far behind again would be the Himalaya! My companion had
already climbed some of these peaks, and I envied him.
But after four years of dreams, of hope, of desire, the
Barre des Ecrins gave me for one day all that a boy's
heart could need.

Many other climbs followed, but none gave me equal
pleasure, right up to 1941 when the "great dream" took
shape in my head. I was at that time instructor at the
mountain school "Jeunesse et Montagne," and we used
to do climbs from the Couvercle hut. For ten days and
more I had the north face of the Grandes Jorasses con-

stantly before my eyes. Little by little the tremendous desire filled my being. To live, youth must guard some secret in its heart.

In 1942 I obtained my release and passed my guide's examination. I lived at Chamonix. Every summer I would do fifty or so climbs, all of them fascinating, but only, as it seemed to me, a prelude. At the school head-quarters of "Jeunesse et Montagne," to which I was attached, the best guides in the valley gave me valuable advice on life in the mountains, on the lore of snow and wind and stars. I was no longer an observant spectator, I was part with the mountains and the elements as a man is part with his country. In the autumn and spring I returned to train on the Calanques cliffs. Cassin and his companions had succeeded where others had failed, because they were expert in the technique of artificial climbing. By this I mean that when a slab is without the smallest hold, when an overhang is too ... overhanging, shall we say, as is often the case on the Walker Spur, the climber can still overcome them, thanks to so-called artificial methods, that is to say with pitons or iron pegs. The Italians had first employed this technique in the

Dolomites; and I, like many other Frenchmen, learned it on the high limestone cliffs between Marseilles and Cassis.

—

At three o'clock in the morning our lantern threw a glimmer over the snow waste of the Leschaux glacier. It was cold, a good sign. We walked quickly, and our feet crunched into the frozen snow. I felt happy. Now the long-awaited day was about to dawn! In front of us, silhouetting their black mass against the star-studded night, the Grandes Jorasses overwhelmed us with their bulk. Each time I looked upwards I felt awed by their vastness. Soon, to-day, to-morrow, and the day after, we would be clinging to that wall. What a contrast between our tiny flickering lantern and this immense cube of frozen rock! But as we approached, my professional task absorbed my thoughts: finding the way in the dark, jumping or turning the crevasses, knotting the rope.

On our right, day was breaking: now was the coldest hour of the night, without colour or shadow, the hour when the steel of an ice-axe sticks to the fingers. We passed the bergschrund and climbed the rib of ice-covered rocks rising from the glacier. High up, the first rays of sunlight were flashing through the gaps in the ridge. Frendo cut steps across the traverse, then I took over the lead. While the rope ran out behind me, I gradually felt my mastery of this world of rock. I experienced a secret joy: my body was fit and my spirit rejoiced at the realization of its dream; for was I not on the Walker Spur? My movements were precise, efficient. I climbed a hundred feet, then Frendo joined me and I went on again. This manœuvre was to be continually repeated over the days to follow, a continual alternation of solitude and company. We were two men on a vertical wall, who chanced to meet from time to time, as the hazard of our rope-lengths dictated.

Soon we came to the first serious difficulty—a great barrier of slabs lined with widely spaced, thin cracks. The climbing of it was a delectable sport, but alas, my enjoyment was a little spoilt by the pair of espadrilles (rope-soled shoes for climbing rocks) which I was wearing and which did not grip. But I was so happy on that day that even this misfortune did not seriously affect me. I climbed, I linked my movements rhythmically, my hands and feet found holds which seemed to have been long intended for their use. I felt just right, and this gave me a great sensation of calm. In an hour the 100-foot crack had been climbed and my companion was having his turn on it; he recovered the pitons which I had fixed, and joined me.

We traversed the icy ledges, and after three rope-lengths reached the foot of the "250-foot corner." It was beautiful in its sheer simplicity, just two slabs arranged like an open book or the angle of a wall, but 250 feet high with two overhangs, one at 80, the other at 160 feet. Here then was the great moment, so long awaited: I was about to climb the great corner of the direct route. To do this I had lightened as far as possible my clumsy human frame; there between my legs were 1,300 feet of space, but they did not weigh me down. At times the granite was so compact that I had to employ artificial aids to make progress. Then, when I reached the rope's end, I planted a piton and attached myself to it. I pulled up the sacks and helped Frendo, whose job was to recover the precious iron pegs as he climbed up to me. When he had joined me he placed himself in the last awkward position possible, with one foot on a tiny hold, the other in a rope stirrup. Then he gave me a shoulder to gain me another six feet. What a strange human pyramid glued to this overhanging wall! Then we parted company, only to join up again later.

Suddenly, while I was climbing the upper part of the corner, drops of rain began to fall. As so often happens, we had been preoccupied with the very difficult climbing and had not seen the clouds roll up. This was no violent passing storm, but bad weather coming from the west, a really serious affair. In five minutes the beautiful granite was transformed into a slippery sheet, while down the back of the corner there poured a miniature waterfall. I was clutching the rock, my arms stretched high, my sleeves became funnels and my anorak a gutter. I was soon soaked to the skin.

What was to be done? I remained calm as before, knowing that on such slippery rock I must climb with double strength. At this point the corner narrowed to a chimney. I climbed "in opposition": that is to say I stuck to the rock with the friction of my feet and back, which pushed in opposite directions as if to widen the gap. My espadrilles, flat against the vertical slab, divided the streaming water like the prow of a ship, as I continued climbing to reach the stance. I felt very sad; all was over for that day. No Jorasses, no Walker Spur, nothing to do but go home. As we could not find the smallest ledge, this involved three long rappels of over 80 feet each, down the 250-foot corner which we had just climbed with such difficulty. In a flash all our prolonged effort was wasted. Meanwhile it started snowing, the sodden ropes froze and stiffened.

At the foot of the corner there was a small platform, suspended as it were from the wall. We swept away the snow with which it was plastered. It was now 7 P.M. and this must be our bivouac site. We drove in two pitons and attached ourselves to them for the night. Meanwhile the snow slowly covered everything, gradually sapping our vitality. Huddled in dumb misery upon our minute rectangle of sloping rock, we had lost not only the Walker Spur but even the desire to climb.

Falling ceaselessly and without sound, the snow seemed to be imposing a perpetual silence around us. It is hard to endure the clinging of clothes, first soaked, then frozen into the stiffness of armour, and the chattering of teeth; to get used to moving one's feet about to avoid frost-bite, to delicate movements undertaken to remove snow piled up between one's back and the wall, ensuring that as little as possible goes down the neck. It is not easy to force oneself to sing in order not to fall asleep....

In the early morning the weather was still bad. That meant a return down the spur, now frozen hard like sheets on a clothes-line some January morning. It meant interminable descents by rappel down frozen ropes, and one involuntary glissade, in which Frendo quickly checked and held me. It meant the glacier, the hut, headquarters of "Jeunesse et Montagne," where I was late back. I had not asked for leave, for fear that it might not be granted. If I had succeeded I would merely have been reprimanded for my lateness. As it was I was informed that I must be punished. Yet what did it matter? There are some days when nothing can touch you. Certainly I regretted our forced retreat, but I was by no means downcast. Come what might, I had gripped between my fingers the wonderful granite of the Walker Spur. The whole adventure had been fascinating: apart from the difficulty of the climb, I had just learned what a nasty spot of trouble can be like on the Jorasses. We had had a good fight and we had given up, not through any failure on our part as climbers, but because of the weather. Some have been stopped by slab or overhang, others have died upon the face. We came back safely from it. And during my eight days "confined to barracks" I promised myself that I would go back. My dream still lived within me.

We had to wait two years for the wall to be in condition once more. For north faces, cold and icebound as they are, attract and hold the snow more than any others. They see so little sun! However, at last, on 14th July 1945, we returned to the attack. This time I had no fears. As two years before, but with greater assurance, we slipped out of the Leschaux hut to stride off into the night. Frendo remained pessimistic, but my optimism was enough for both.

Two years ago we had tried out our strength, but this time we wanted to succeed. I knew very well that other climbers were after this climb that day. Of course the mountains do not change, they are always beautiful, not just to the eye, but above all to the heart. The Walker Spur is still the most serious undertaking in the Alps, but I had dreamed about this face too much these several years past to be satisfied by the climb alone. I wanted to experience the sense of discovery. For in every climb there is more than just the act of climbing and the view: there is also the mystery. Thus, while it was true that Cassin, Esposito, and Tizzoni had made the first ascent seven years before, yet the charm of the face was still almost as if it had remained virgin. What did Cassin signify here? We knew nothing of him, except that he was very strong, the outstanding climber of the Dolomites. Here he did no more than get up. Yet were another climber from my own country to climb the face, he would destroy the mystery for me. It was not just a few pitons hammered into the walls that would make the Jorasses less beautiful; the charm would continue, but it would be veiled. Sometimes a flower will wilt at a mere touch of the hand.

Meanwhile the sky was clear, a pale darkness. That meant good weather. We found the point of attack, then climbed on from stance to stance: the rock rib, the snow slope, the traverse, the first barrier of slabs. I was in splendid form, enjoying the sensation of expending the minimum effort required to climb; as though my strength was concealed and I was now paying out from a boundless reservoir of energy stored over the years.

We reached the little platform that had been the site

of our bivouac; there was nothing there now but a bit of silver paper. I seemed to see again the whiteness of that night we had spent there. I heard the muffled noises, the stones rattling down the couloir, the snow that fell so lightly one would have said it was stage decoration. It had been an endless night, a night which brought no sun with its passing. But to-day the sky was so light that you could almost see the stars behind.

Above us rose the 250-foot corner. Climbing it now was pure joy, and at its top we were at the end of the ground we knew. Here was our last piton, a welcome landmark on our way. And here we ought to eat, for we had swallowed nothing since three o'clock in the morning and it was now 1 P.M. But the bread and chocolate which we tried to chew refused to go down, and our eyes were fixed up there, on the great slabs of the Grey Tower. Quickly we set off again. Climbing and confidence go hand in hand. We continued to climb till nightfall.

At nine in the evening we prepared our bivouac on a minute wrinkle in the Grey Tower: a tiny ledge, but it was a joy to find; we had seen nothing like it for hours. It was hardly large enough to sit on, with our legs dangling over the great central couloir. There, more or less seated and hooked on to our pitons, we passed a painful and cold, but exciting night. For were we not on the Walker Spur? Besides, it was cold, and that meant good weather! We climbed on upwards in the morning, stiff and awkward over the icy rocks. The difficulty was very great, for we were up against the smooth slabs of the Grey Tower. Yesterday we had turned its base, thanks to a rising traverse. We had climbed like ants round a tree, on the bark, but now the bark had thinned out. Each rope-length, each yard, each step, was a constant problem. My body, my life, the whole of my being must be adapted to and transformed by this hard, indifferent rock. For we must match the unremitting rock with the efficiency of our technique and the power of our will.

I remember specially one overhanging crack, a light sabre-cut that split the bulging rock. It was plainly repellent, but I had tried everywhere else and there was nothing, not even a crack. This then was the only solution. Frendo called to me from below, but what was I to say to him? The rope is a wonderful thing for the feeling of unity that it gives, and yet up here, attacking this crack and climbing it, I felt quite alone. There was my companion, sixty-five feet below me. What a fall I would have if I slipped! For the rope behind me, splendid as it was, would be useless. But I could not climb without it, without the friendliness it transmitted. It gave me courage. So I started off, my whole body thrown backward by the overhang, holding to the rock by my hands, jammed and clenched in the crack. I tried to move quickly, for the climbing was very athletic, but my feet gripped poorly, their hold was slight, precarious, yet vital. My body bent back under the overhang, my hands grasped, fingers curled, they *must* hold in the crack…

When I reached the stance and Frendo joined me, there were more slabs and more cracks ahead. It was not till 3 P.M. that we reached the top of the Grey Tower. Our first feeling was of thirst, for we had drunk nothing since the evening before. We would be hungry if we were not so thirsty. Frendo, who had set off to reconnoitre the left side of the spur, where a little snow might still be clinging, returned joyfully brandishing a flask full of water. Alas! his movements were *too* joyful, and the wet aluminum flask slipped from between his fingers. At that moment we suffered the supreme sense of helplessness; we had held this flask, which contained our desire; now we saw it fall and bounce, then we saw it no longer but heard it still and could imagine it disappearing into space. Then all around was still, indifferent.

The biscuits and chocolate, in fact everything that we tried to eat, dried our throats a little more. We spat them out and took up our sacks again. Fortunately the climbing continued to be very fine and, though rather less difficult, sufficiently delicate to keep us occupied. Towards the middle of the afternoon we arrived under the great step at a height of about 13,000 feet. Once again we had to exert ourselves to the utmost. After an ice couloir and a triangular patch of snow we were stopped by a chimney composed of friable rock. Frendo, more accustomed to bad rock than I, made the first attempt. He traversed twelve feet to my right, then started up the chimney. He drove in a piton, which looked as though it would not hold. At last he was almost at the top, attempting to get a position above a great jammed block which formed an overhang fifty feet above my head. For a moment he hesitated, then he made his decisive move. Just at the moment of achievement I saw him lurch backwards with the block in his arms. His fall lasted the space of a lightning flash, yet to me it all seemed to be happening very slowly. At such moments brain and action are amazingly swift and incisive. As soon as I saw him go I drew in the rope between us very quickly, so as to limit the length of his fall. Then, when he passed my level a little to the right—the piton had not held—I said to myself: "Now I mustn't pull in the rope between us any more, or it will go slipping through my fingers and I shan't be able to hold him." Very quickly I slid the rope round a little leaf of rock in front of me, then took some of the slack in my right hand to soften the shock and so that the rope would not break from too abrupt a jerk on contact with the leaf. Everything held. Frendo came to rest about thirty feet below, a total fall of over eighty feet almost entirely through space.

A great stillness followed, broken by only one sound, the noise of the piton hammer, which had slipped from my friend's hand, as it went clattering and bouncing down the wall.

Frendo recovered from the shock and took stock of his fall. He was relatively unhurt, no more than a twist of the left ankle, a scrape of the finger-tips, and a violent pain in the ribs caused by the jerk of the rope which had held him. He rejoined me as best he could, and we did what we could for his injuries. Then I handed the ropes to him and quietly took over the lead again. Obviously it was not worth trying to get up where my companion had just fallen, so I made out to the left across a slab. The difficulty was extreme, and to add to it the rock was wet with a thin rain which had just begun to fall. I am not exaggerating when I say that a square inch or two less of hold on this slab and I would never have got up. As it was I reached a little platform, drove in a piton, and secured my companion as well as I could. All these manœuvres had lost us a lot of time; it was now eight o'clock and we must bivouac on the spot. There followed an unpleasant night, especially for Frendo.

In the early dawn we resumed the climb; from the start it was extremely difficult, vertical and terribly exposed. We climbed in a light mist, but we experienced a great joy, a rather savage joy; it was, I believe, the recognition of the urge that every man feels deep within himself—the urge at least once in a lifetime to exceed his limits. Meanwhile the summit was getting nearer; despite the mist we felt it very close. At midday on the third day we climbed out through the final cornice, and found ourselves on the summit of the Grandes Jorasses, the Pointe Walker.

So it is that from our dreams are born the great joys of life. But dreams we must have, and all the time. I prefer dreams to memories.

2. THE CENTRAL SPUR

Two years after our ascent of the direct route up the north spur of the Pointe Walker, the Grandes Jorasses were to provide me with a second great joy.

It was the beginning of the season. With Jean Franco I was directing the course of instruction for guides at the National Ski and Mountaineering School. The profession of guide is regulated, and rightly so, by stages. One must first of all be a porter, then do a national course for a month. Each day the aspirant guides are marked for their skill on ice and rock, for their route-finding, their confidence, resolution, coolness and so on. That year the level of the aspirants was very high. We had just achieved some of the really great routes: Mont Blanc by the Red Sentinel and Route Major, the traverse of the Aiguilles du Diable, the north face of the Pain de Sucre, the Dent du Requin by the Mayer-Dibona route, the north ridge of the Aiguille de Leschaux. The enthusiasm and competence of these aspirants prompted me to put into execution another of my plans, that of taking a team from the guides' course up the central spur of the Grandes Jorasses, first climbed by the Germans. This route had only been repeated four times, and never by a French party. For us it was still full of mystery.

So it came about that on 4th July 1947, after having weighed the idea for more than a month, I made my decision. We were to attack the north face with a party of seven divided into three ropes: Georges Michel and myself, Vergez and Muller, Lachenal[1] (later to reach the top of Annapurna with Maurice Herzog), Bréchut and Revel. I led the first rope, Vergez the second, Lachenal the third.

At 5 A.M. we were passing the bergschrund. At seven o'clock we had reached the first tower, at eight o'clock the second. The whole way up the climb I took a host of precautions. No less than ten times we joined up to make only one rope of seven, over six hundred feet long, so as to reduce the risks to the minimum. Despite the handicap of our numbers, we emerged on the summit ridge at the Pointe Michel Croz at ten o'clock on the

[1]Killed in a skiing accident on the Glacier du Géant, 1955.

evening of 4th July, whereas previous parties, although much lighter, had had to bivouac on the face. Night had fallen, but on the Italian side there was a moon.

The whole way up this route, I experienced on that day one of the truest delights of my profession, the brotherhood of the guides. Shortly after my return I opened Joseph Conrad's *Youth* and read this sentence, which is as applicable to mountains and guides and guides-to-be as it is to the sea and sailors: "Between the five of us there was the strong bond of the sea, and also the fellowship of the craft, which no amount of enthusiasm for yachting, cruising and so on can give, since one is only the amusement of life and the other is life itself."[1]

A short time after, however, as we sat down to bivouac on a comfortable terrace on the south or Italian side, a great block detached itself somehow from the summit ridge thirty feet above our heads, struck us from behind and sent Georges Michel, the "aspirant" on my left, and myself hurtling down into the darkness below. Not knowing how or why, I found myself thirty feet lower down, jammed in a rock chimney in a perfect climbing

[1]From the opening page of *Youth* by Joseph Conrad (J. M. Dent & Sons Ltd.).

position, feet against one wall, back against the other. I knew nothing at all about it, but my reflexes must have acted on their own. During my fall I must have put out my arms to stop myself.

My friends called, and I answered them. They threw me down a rope and I tied myself on. I had a severe pain in the knees and chest, for in fact my knee-cap, left foot, and one rib were broken. As they pulled me to help me up to them I heard them shouting "Michel, Michel!" There was no reply, and I said to myself: "He's dead." After a very painful night and a delicate descent, we found the aspirant guide Georges Michel next day, fifteen hundred feet lower, on the glacier. The expression on his face was serene. The morning before, as we started up the spur, he had said to me: "Gaston, think of doing the north face of the Grandes Jorasses! I've dreamed of this all my life." And he had added with a laugh: "After, I don't mind dying."

The chain of Mont Blanc is on the frontier. But high hills are a bond and not a dividing rampart. It is impossible to praise the devotion with which the Courmayeur guides came to our rescue, the spontaneity with which they and their compatriots helped us. Indeed it is good to recall how that comradeship of the guides, which we had experienced so joyously on the climb, was confirmed in less happy circumstances beyond the frontiers; for the guides, whether from Chamonix or Courmayeur, are all one family. And whenever I now climb routes on the Italian side of Mont Blanc, I think of that rescue. It is more than a memory, it is the seal of a deep comradeship.

THE NORTH-EAST FACE OF PIZ BADILE

The Piz Badile is situated in the most enchanting cirque of mountains that one could imagine, the Bondasca Valley in the Ticino. Here everything is wonderfully ordered, from the depths of the valley to the slender summits of pale granite. And the villages of Promontogno and Bondo are real mountain villages, a mixture of Swiss orderliness and Italian fantasy: not ugly, hybrid growths of upstart towns, as is often the case with mountaineering and skiing centres.

The path which leads towards the summits cuts deeply through the dense, scented forest. When you have crossed the moss-clad ravines you reach a vast amphitheatre of mountains. Here peace reigns. The only sound, the only movement, is that of the torrents and waterfalls, born from the womb of the eternal glaciers as they go rushing down noisily through this world of silence, whose only life is the slow rhythm of the seasons. Wild gorges open up on either side: deep and twisted, worn and polished smooth each spring by the avalanches, they are sprinkled with dead trees tossed among the bushes that are reborn each summer. It is a romantic scene. Here you are tempted to sit and gaze and drink it in. The air is laden with a delicious scent of grass, of resin and of the keen breeze. Here a man forgets everything, even that he has come to climb.

The Piz Badile is of modest height, no more than 10,853 feet. It is not surrounded by huge glaciers, nor are the neighbouring summits imposing. But its northeast face presents a wall 3,000 feet high, smooth and straight and regular to perfection. Moreover, like many other mountain groups, the Piz Badile and its neighbours, the Piz Cengalo, Pizzi Gemelli and Aiguilles de Sciora, form the frontier between Switzerland to the north and Italy to the south. As is the case with the Grandes Jorasses, the north faces are as difficult as their sunlit southern flanks are easy and attractive.

—

Here again it was Riccardo Cassin who, after his great climbs in the Dolomites on the Torre Trieste and the western Cima (peak) di Lavaredo, was attracted by the wall of the Badile. After a first visit to reconnoitre the face Cassin and his climbing companions, Esposito and Ratti, made an attempt in earnest on the first day of fine weather, 13th July 1937. At the same time two young climbers from Como, Molteni and Valsecchi, were attempting the wall from a different starting-point. The two parties spent the night together on a little platform, and on the next day Molteni and Valsecchi showed signs of fatigue. During the rainy days that had preceded their attempt they had remained at the Sciora hut under difficult conditions, sleeping on the kitchen floor because they did not have the key to the dormitory, and eating sparingly so that they would be ready to start out at a moment's notice. Accordingly they joined on to Cassin's rope.

On the evening of the second day the climbers

bivouacked at the foot of the big, light-coloured slab. It was a bad night, for a storm had risen, and on the next day the rocks were in very bad condition. At last, thanks to the determination and immense powers of resistance of Cassin, Esposito and Ratti, the five climbers emerged on the summit at 4 P.M. on the third day, in the teeth of a blizzard. Then they began the descent by the normal route, down the Italian side. This is quite simple in good conditions, but now the whirling snow and gusts of icy wind made it very hard going. Almost immediately Molteni died of exhaustion. The others continued their painful way, but when they had reached the last obstacle, a little rock wall, the visibility was so limited, the rocks so unrecognizable under their coating of snow, that Cassin hesitated, casting about for the right way. If they could only cross or get round this rock step they would be saved, for the Gianetti hut was very close. Cassin plunged out, then after a short while came back again. The four climbers stood together, and Valsecchi, who had not seen his friend's death, looked round for Molteni. He realized what had happened and burst into tears; then he too sank down and died. Like many another mountain, the Badile had seen to it that victory was dearly won. For twelve years the north-east face of the Badile was abandoned. The great difficulty, the distance and the circumstances surrounding the first ascent scared mountaineers away. Why then was I attracted by it? There are ideas which link together, flow on and gradually impose themselves. Basically it is a question of wanting a thing enough; and if your desire is a worthy one it will be granted in the long run. But the ripe fruit must be plucked, and there is a special pleasure in savouring the fruit of desire gathered in due season. So it was with the Badile.

In 1945, on the Walker Spur of the Grandes Jorasses, I had followed a climb first made by Cassin; so it was again this time. On the former route I had known nothing whatever about the line he had taken. Again, here on the Badile, I knew almost nothing of the route he had followed; I had the benefit of a technical note, but was handicapped by the situation of the mountain, in a district isolated and unknown to me. Thus it became a matter of recapturing the spirit of Cassin himself at the foot of his great climb, his will to conquer and his love of the game. Given these qualities the rest follows, all the delights of climbing and the eventual triumph.

On the eve of a great climb, and especially before the Walker, I have often tried to recapture the feelings of a climber on the eve of a first ascent, simply for the hard, egotistical pleasure of pioneering; but first for the pleasure of prowling about at the foot of the great slabs, of looking at them with a kind of tenderness, making out their forms, knowing them, savouring them in advance. First the joy of anticipation, then the delight of action. All this there was. And yet in itself the prospect of the climbing would not have sufficed; for a good technique combined with fitness is all that is needed to overcome the difficulties. This time there was another pleasure to add to the rest: the chance to test the mastery of my craft and to observe the delight of my friend Bernard Pierre during the three days we would spend together on the Badile. "Right! Let's go." His look of relief had been sufficient reward for the long periods of deliberations and doubt, when I had to weigh carefully the difficulties of the climb, to balance desire against cold reason and conscience. Was it reasonable to tackle the central spur of the Jorasses north face with learners? Was it now sensible to take Bernard to the Badile, with his brief experience of mountains?

Originally there had been no such doubts, for I was to have made the attempt with Jean Deudon. It would have been a splendid symbol of our friendship. We would have gone, and together we would have looked upon, then loved these great slabs. We would have attacked; Jean would have taken the big sack and as usual would have given me a shoulder where necessary. What a fine pedestal those shoulders of his were! We would have bivouacked, and as usual we would have been rained on and stormed on, but I would not have dared to say anything, for as usual Jean would not have complained. He would only have asked for cigarettes to warm his enormous frame. Perhaps we would have talked; he would have said:

"You know, at Camp IV on Hidden Peak[1]..."

On the next day we would have set off again, now one now the other leading, and I would have felt strong

[1] Hidden Peak, 26,470 feet, is near K2 in the Karakoram, and at the time of writing has not yet been climbed. Deudon was a member of the French expedition which attempted to climb it under H. de Ségogne in 1936.

enough to climb pitches of the seventh or eighth degree of severity, having with me the indomitable Jean Deudon. But this time the weather had decided differently. I had to wait, then choose the moment, and as Jean was not there, what could be more natural than to take Bernard Pierre? At Easter we had traversed the Aiguilles du Diable[1]. And a short while before we had all three been on the rope together on the great face of the Aiguille de la Brenva[2].

Only the previous evening at supper we had been wondering what to do in the fine weather which had at last begun three days before, during this particularly rainy summer. We felt the need for a big climb, something in the nature of an expedition even. It is amusing to recall the bubbling optimism which reigns over these evening meals. We had been depressed, but now the stars had come back and out we went to look at them, to receive their message. We came in again joyful, but scarcely

[1] A row of five small, very sharp rocky pinnacles (the highest 13,481 feet) on the flank of one of the buttresses of Mont Blanc. First traversed throughout by Armand Charlet and party in 1928.

[2] A peak on the Brenva side of Mont Blanc, 10,742 feet. One of the lower peaks available from Courmayeur, first climbed in 1898. The hardest route on it is that made up the east face by G. Rébuffat, B. Pierre and J. Deudon, 1948.

were we seated than we were nervous once more: were they still shining? We went to sleep happy, and yet we would have liked to stay awake with these cold stars in which our hopes rested. The night was lightened by a new fire, and our awakening made happy by the thought of settled fine weather.

Off we go then!

During the morning I had to climb the Brévent[1] by the face, and in the early afternoon the Gaillands[2], both with clients. As usual I only finished packing my sack as I started running for the *téléférique*. But I was in a good mood, and if the client was not a good goer, so much the worse for him! This hesitant client of mine was losing me precious time in this limited spell of fine weather!

Meanwhile Bernard had prepared the sacks, and there was the car waiting for us. Good-bye, Clocher-Clochertons, Brévent, Gaillands, on which I had been scrambling for the past week between the showers. I felt a kind of fatherly affection for them now. It was five o'clock as we drove off, without any notion where we would spend the night. But when you are happy

[1] Mountain of 8,285 feet near Chamonix.
[2] Crags near Chamonix, used for practice climbs.

that does not worry you overmuch. Nor, for that matter, could we foretell where we should be bivouacking in two and three days' time, tied to the wall of the Badile.

The evening before we were talking of nothing but the Matterhorn by the Furggen ridge; we did not so much as mention the Badile, for Promontogno seemed too distant and the fine weather too recent. But since waking up that morning I had felt good-humoured, my thoughts wandered, and I was happy; my plan of last winter, the Badile, had crept back into my head. The Badile! Who named these mountains? We had just had a fortnight in the Dolomites, and the mere sound of their names already filled the soul with longing. And now Promontogno, Sciora, Badile—these were singing through our heads.

This new idea put everything into the melting-pot again. It had all been so simple before. I had already done the Furggen, and it was a fine memory. But at Visp we had to make up our minds, and instead of turning right for Zermatt and the Matterhorn, we continued along the valley of the Rhône, along the great road bordered with poplars, heading eastwards. Beside me I could sense Bernard's eagerness, as on the eve of a great battle.

The Sciora hut was burnt during the war, and we slept between the coarse linen sheets of the *pension* near by. It is like a very well-kept old inn. At half past three next morning the mistress of the house, stout and kindly, brought us our ham sandwiches and sent us on our way with a "Buona fortuna" before shutting the heavy door behind us. Then a workman engaged on building the new hut accompanied us as we walked up. Lantern in hand, he showed us the route that he followed each day; and I thought of Cassin, eleven years before, climbing up to explore this untouched face.…

By the time we arrived at the foot of the wall it was half past eight. On the right we could identify the line of attack of the two climbers from Como, and for a moment we were tempted to go left, to the foot of the great central couloir. But the sun, warming the higher part of the face, started stones falling; they came tumbling down to smudge the little glacier below. We put on the rope and shared out the loads; whenever possible I would be climbing with a very light sack. Bernard's sack was very much heavier.

The glacier was very low, and the initial slabs were worn smooth. We looked for and found the snow bridge over the gap. Just as I began to cross it, it collapsed, much to the amusement of the workman, who had stayed to watch us start. This made the take-off very delicate, and in the end Bernard gave me a shoulder, following after himself. We then went on together, following a long shelf as far as the first open corner. This brought us up with a start, for up to here it had been easy. We climbed it and found other upward shelves, bringing us leftwards to the foot of a great block detached from the face. This was a real turning-point, for it is here that the north-east face of the Piz Badile begins in earnest.

It is a repulsive place; but higher up a piton in the rock showed me the route. While Bernard passed the gear up to me, I looked up at these open corners rising in diagonals towards the left: one angled like a roof, the other convex, almost vertical, flattening out one hundred and fifty feet below us. I could not help thinking of Cassin arriving at this point, and immediately starting to climb this difficult section as naturally as he had overcome the easy shelves. Undoubtedly these Dolomite climbers are lucky to be constantly "ready for anything"—in a frame of mind which accepts everything that comes: slanting corners and repellent overhangs; traverses followed by drops of hundreds of feet *en rappel*; the lack of stances and stances on pitons; passages where progress is at the rate of thirty feet an hour, or where the only solution is to swing across the void, although you can only see some fifteen feet ahead. Yet one thing was surprising and rather deceptive about this cliff, in contrast with the Dolomites. These slabs, these corners of splendid granite, are less steep and less exposed than the limestone corners; but despite this it is impossible to climb them without pitons, for the rock is too compact, lacking even the smallest hold. There were no airy hundred-foot drops as on the Sass Pordoï or the Spigolo Giallo in the Dolomites, where the rope behind me hung free of the rock. Here the stirrups did not hang, they lay against the slabs. Yet this slanting corner was difficult; you needed to hammer in the pitons with the left hand, and the cracks overlapped downwards. You had to trust a piton driven in upside-down, then a second fixed in the same way. I found this piton work tedious and exhausting, and did not like it at all. It was not so much the fact of leaving those easy shelves behind, or of reckoning that a return would be almost impossible down those slanting corners; but it seemed so futile to be doing nothing but hammer in pegs. Climbing one corner after another, I advanced thirty feet an hour up this wall of three thousand feet—a ridiculous pace. It had been all very well putting in a piton or two in the slabs on the east face of the Crocodile[1]. But what was the point of fastening myself here, in fine weather, to a series of little nails?

And yet, absorbed perhaps by the technical interest, I found myself choosing the right piton from my supply, driving it into the rock, hearing it sing as it went in, and confiding my whole body, with all that it contains of hope and love, to this one iron peg. I gained just three feet, and my interest grew. I redoubled my efforts to pass the angle of the corner, which was no longer sloping but vertical; I lengthened myself and stretched out to gain another few inches. I found another crack for a bent "extra-flat" piton. At last it was firmly fixed, and with the help of the stirrups another six feet were gained. I could no longer see Bernard, but he could judge of my advance from the noise of the pitons and the least movement of the ropes.

[1] One of the Chamonix Aiguilles, 11,942 feet high.

There between my feet the slabs swept away, not quite vertical but curved three hundred feet below like a ski-jumping hill. Thanks to a few holds I was able to climb without pitons, and reached the next stance more quickly. I hauled up the big sack on the third rope, and Bernard climbed with the small one. Then it was my turn to feel *him* climb up, from the tremors of the ropes. He recovered the pitons, a tiring, acrobatic feat in itself, and brought them up to me. These iron pegs at least provide the excuse for a smile between second and leader, when the former hands them over. On I went, the richer by all my ironmongery and a smile. The hammering of pitons continued.

There followed more corners and more slabs, till we arrived at last at the bivouac site of the Italians; but we did not halt here. The route slants very steeply upwards to the left, over fine slabs with firm, small holds. It was sheer joy to be climbing without artificial aid once more. On we went, stance after stance, rope-length by rope-length, until we reached the little snow-field half-way up the face. Here the Badile seems to lie back, only to soar again in a fresh upward surge. It was now a quarter past 6 P.M., and I left the sack in order to have a look at the way ahead. There is little relief in this immense sweep of smooth slabs; everything is so sloping that we wondered under which of these projecting eaves Cassin could have squeezed himself.

Once again, as at the beginning of the climb, I was tempted by the great central couloir, ninety feet to the left; but the stones, icicles and waterfall which came crashing down it soon scared me off. I skirted under the wall and found Cassin's corner topped by an enormous overhang; there lay the way. But for that evening we were only making a reconnaissance. It was now half past six, and 28th August, on a face long deserted by the sun. It was clearly too late to think of starting on this next step, but I climbed the first, very difficult hundred feet, planted pitons and returned to Bernard. Night was creeping up.

We went down a further seventy feet and prepared our bivouac. It was fine and cold. Despite the gathering darkness we took our time over settling in, so as to shorten the long hours of the night as much as possible. We planted the piton anchoring us to the rock, and put on our eiderdown jackets[1]. We gratefully unfolded the wind-proof smocks which we had hesitated to bring the

---

[1] The French use the word *duvet* for these jackets.

evening before. We lit the candle and the solid meta-fuel stove. For us two human beings the face of Piz Badile was home for the night.

After this performance we looked at our watches. It was still only eight o'clock, and a long night of sleepless inactivity lay ahead. Tensed with cold, hooked on to the Badile by a piton like pictures hanging on a wall, we endured only for the sunshine to come. The sky was beautiful. But among high mountains the chilly dawn is very slow in arriving. As the wall faces north-east we had hoped that we might receive the early rays to help us start. But when the sun did appear it dallied three hundred feet above our heads, and we decided to climb up towards it. The snow was hard and the frost had made ice of what had melted the day before. At eight o'clock we were at the foot of the open corner. Stiff from cold, I climbed clumsily with the help of the rope left yesterday. But thirty feet higher I was touching rock white and warm with the sun; the vitality which had ebbed from my body sprang out anew, my movements flowed more easily and my pace quickened. Down below Bernard was still shivering, but I reached the stance quickly and brought him up. Then I passed him the ropes and went on.

The morning before we had been surprised by these corners; to-day I marvelled at the audacity of such a route. The ground here is as vertical as a limestone cliff and the climbing airy as you could wish. There is only just the bare minimum to allow you to get up. It was not a succession of slabs that we were climbing, but one immense slab, all but perfect in its regularity and smoothness. Everything about the climbing of it was a joy, and as we climbed I seemed to understand the meaning of our exploit. It was not the increasing nearness of the summit, or the climb in itself, that filled us with a quiet joy, but the feeling that mind and muscles were fulfilling their intended function. Somehow we were "in the right place."

What pleasure Cassin must have had tracing his route up this wall! The certainty of being able to get up must have given him the strength to ignore the awesome aspect of the overhangs above. To reach them we had to climb a thin crack up a sheer sweep of wall leading right up under the overhang. Then we must depend on pitons fixed head downwards, and step in stirrups hanging out over the void, in order to traverse horizontally to the left, under the eaves, and gain the corner that follows.

The manœuvre is almost simple, for there is no alternative. Then the corner itself was long and difficult; the ropes did not run easily, for they tended to jam under the eaves. The exit was delicate, on rounded holds, and our hundred-foot length of rope only just allowed me to reach the tiny ledge which served as stance. Then there was the tiresome strain of pulling up the sacks, and Bernard started up, again performing feats of acrobatics as he recovered the pitons. Soon he emerged beside me, handing me triumphantly the precious metal so that I might use it yet again.

The huge scale of the cliff was brought home forcibly to us at this point by the height that we had gained. After a delicate climb up a wall I reached a minute ledge by a tiny crack, the ledge on which the Italians had made their second bivouac. So the great buttress had been overcome! Above us was a large, light-coloured slab, very recognizable from the description; and on our right the start of the crack by which we must climb it. But it was mid-day, and we stopped to eat on this platform of sad memories. Usually pitons simply mark a route, but on bivouac sites they convey a feeling of joy or sadness. Here men sang because they were cold; here they ate, not because they were hungry, but to keep up their failing strength, before they left this terrace for a night their bodies had warmed.

But we could not linger; dark clouds now covered the sky. We started up the crack, which, higher up, widens into a cleft and finishes on the north ridge. The climbing was delicate without being difficult, for crack and cleft were drenched by streams of water from the melting snow-fields above. We climbed with care, but we had to hurry too, for the bad weather that invariably accompanies big climbs seemed to be getting worse around us; the clouds darkened, the light faded, the rock appeared flat and featureless. Horrified at the thought of a storm in this fissure, where the sheet of water would so soon be transformed into a torrent, I climbed fast, very fast, and rather roughly. Behind me the ropes were heavy with moisture. Above, the cleft was barred by vertical walls forming a difficult obstacle, demanding care and attention. Meanwhile the rock grew greasy under its film of water. It began to rain, but we seemed to be making our way through a curtain of vapour, frigid almost tangible and hard to penetrate. There was nothing ethereal about these regions, and yet I felt myself as light as if I had abandoned my human frame; I almost ran up the rocks. A stream of water flowed from the holds to which I was clinging, trickled down my arm and froze me to the shoulder, which was already soaked by the rope running over it as I secured Bernard. Bernard climbed very fast, and we gained height rapidly. But this couloir which had looked so short from Cassin's bivouac, was in fact over six hundred feet high; that meant seven or eight rope-lengths, and that is a lot of rope to be handling.

Luckily there was a brief clearing of the weather, and we made use of it. But higher up the angle steepened and I had to use pitons, which lost us precious time. My thoughts were very clear, despite the anxiety and my state of exaltation. I was afraid of the storm and used all my strength to hammer the pitons into the cracks. Meanwhile Bernard, who had been carrying the big sack, was now burdened with mine as well. When he hoisted himself up by the soaking rope to gain time, a little fountain bubbled down his sleeves. Once, looking up, he said:

"If only Mother could see me now!"

Alas! the clearing did not last long; the rain began to fall more heavily. Fortunately I had just surmounted the last steep rise and had reached a ledge. While securing Bernard I tried to study the ground ahead, but visibility was limited to a few yards. I sensed that we were at the level of the sloping shelf which must be followed to the left when one leaves the couloir. It was very tempting to continue straight up towards the north ridge, but in bad weather this couloir may become a trap. For a moment we hesitated before launching out along the shelf, which is very narrow. We thought of Cassin, held up by bad conditions and by his large party, but still determined not to abandon the face. At this moment the storm burst, and we were afraid of the waterfall coming down the gully. It was only five o'clock, and if we had gone on we would just have had the time to reach the summit that evening.

I traversed eighty feet along the shelf, which widened but was coated with snow. The storm became violent. Just as Bernard joined me there was a flash of lightning, very close. As there was no rock spike I drove in a piton and we pulled on our smocks. To continue was out of the question; there was nothing for it but to wait to see how it would turn out.

It turned out badly. From an inky sky heavy rain pelted down upon us. Between repeated thunderclaps lightning struck very close, blinding us with its dazzling, dread glare and hurting our eyes. We were drenched to the skin, cold to the marrow. Bernard looked at his watch: it was six o'clock. Another bivouac on the face!

Then began an interminable vigil. A respite of ten minutes would have allowed us to advance a little closer to the summit. Yet it was not so much the top that we longed for, as to move a little instead of staying anchored to our piton; to *do* something rather than just wait. Our muscles already felt stiff and cold; the inaction was slowly destroying us. For we were climbers, built for climbing, not to remain stormbound for hours on end. We would gladly climb anything, a chimney, a crack, a slab. We would climb silently, simply climb, stretch out and stand upright. Bernard would feel the wet nylon rope slip between his fingers while I climbed. It need only be one rope-length in our accustomed way. It was not just a whim. It would do us so much good! I would say to Bernard: "I'm at the stance, come on," and he would take the two sacks without complaining of their weight, so thankful would he be to leave this shelf....

But now this dream was no longer possible. It was 7:30 P.M. and there had been no break. Now night was upon us, and we were doomed to the shelf. All around us lightning flashed and a few hailstones fell. Bernard again consulted his watch: the flashes were coming every three minutes, and each time we were afraid. Against the wind which knocks you down and sends you gradually to sleep, against the cold which shrivels you and freezes your blood, against the stinging snow which sows death— against all these the mountaineer can struggle. But the lightning strikes, stiffens and kills at one blow. And each time it whitened the night for a second, we cowered fearful against the rock, mere shadows of life.

How I longed for the snow which falls after a storm, the snow which covers everything in the ensuing calm! I recalled the storm which caught René Mallieux and myself two years before, while we were doing rappels down the Aiguille du Roc[1]. It was six o'clock, at the end

---

[1] A very sharp pinnacle on the side of the Aiguille de Grépon (11,424 feet) above Chamonix.

of September, and we had had to bivouac at the gap. All night it had snowed; we were soaked and frozen, for the light snow penetrated everywhere. Above all we had to be careful not to fall asleep. From time to time I would pull out my hand to sweep away the snow that was cloaking us. By the early morning a foot and a half of fresh snow covered everything. I withdrew my hand, slightly frost-bitten, into a pocket damp with melting snow, and hesitated to take it out again. But I said to myself: "I am the guide, and the guide *must* be invulnerable." With that thought I felt sure that my fingers would not be frost-bitten. But now, faced with lightning, I was miserable and powerless.

The cold held us more and more in its grip. For something to do we decided to make tea. We brought out the stove, set it up as well as we could between us, put the meta-fuel inside the windshield and the snow in the pan. But it was all quite useless, for no sooner had we struck a match than it was blown out by the wind. And when we were lucky enough to light the meta, it was the meta which immediately went out. After using all the matches we remained crouching stupidly over our useless stove, until, to pass the time, Bernard brought out the cigarettes. But as we had no more matches, our craving for a smoke also remained unsatisfied.

The flashes became less frequent. We had the impression that the storm was moving off towards the Bernina, casting a strange light on the lake of Silvaplana. We unbent our legs, stretched them out and let them hang over space. We had been crouching against this rock, motionless on this narrow shelf, for hours! Below us, in a single sweep, the slabs of the Badile swept away unbroken.... Bernard dropped a glove...a few more hailstones fell...we ate a little.... Far off the lightning flickered over St. Moritz.

As the storm moved off we made plans for the morrow. It was still raining and we shivered, but already we were looking ahead. If only the rock was not too wet, if only a ray of sunshine would touch it...for we had still to do a very exposed traverse, whose difficulty was stressed by Cassin in his technical note on the climb. There would be certain precautions to take so as to climb at all; we must wriggle our feet in our boots and rub our limbs. But our clothes, right down to our shirts, were saturated with rain, first warmed by contact with the skin but played on by the wind when we started moving and moulded into a sheet of ice.

Now that the thunder and lightning had moved off, we could hear the stone-falls crashing down the face of the Piz Cengalo (11,056 feet) opposite. But the fireworks of the night before were lacking; they had been a fine display against the blackness of the night. Instinctively we lowered our heads between hunched shoulders, curled our legs under us and tried to stop breathing.... Then the lightning returned; a flash lit up the rocks around, and I could see the rain dripping like milk on Bernard's rounded back and shining hood. I heard a faint noise, like paper being crumpled; then, immediately after, a deafening crash. The whole cirque of mountains around was shaken, the echo rolling from wall to wall.

We had had no more than a respite in the storm. In my misery I felt frightened. Lightning flashed and sizzled around us, the thunder roared. Bernard told me the time: it was just before midnight. The nightmare had been going on for six hours. No sooner did the restful darkness return, our tense, cramped bodies relax, and our fear for a moment release us, than another ball of fire would strike the rock.

Often before we had been shaken, buffeted, tested by storm; we had even been in danger of being dislodged from our holds, but there had always been an outlet in retreat: leaping from rock to rock, down the snow slopes, speeding downwards and losing height rapidly, moving fast and with precision. All this was stimulating. But this night we were not on the move. We must content ourselves with simply being there, anchored to the spot.

The night dragged endlessly.

In the early morning, when the storm ceased, we made the horizontal traverse of which Cassin writes in his note. Then two rappels landed us in the great central couloir. There a poorly defined *arête*, sheltered from stone-fall, led to the summit. It was midday when we arrived, to meet two climbers who had come up by the ordinary way on the south flank. After such a struggle we rejoiced in the presence of other humans. Everything tasted new: sun and rock, men, colours, tobacco, and an orange which they offered us. Our gaze ranged over the surrounding peaks. Once more the weather was fine and the mountains inviting. Then together we descended happily by the ordinary way to the Gianetti hut.

I had had the finest reward of all. I had indeed succeeded in doing the Badile as a guide; but above all, and the greatest prize of all in my job, my confidence in my companion was justified. The guide would not be so strong if he did not give something of himself. And Bernard, who had made his début two years before, had now won his spurs on the slabs of the Piz Badile.

THE NORTH FACE OF
THE DRUS

The Montenvers train starts off in a cloud of dust, engages in the rack and begins to climb, jolting its cargo of chattering and sleepy tourists. It dives into a tunnel, then enters another and finally arrives at Caillet, where it halts to water the engine[1]. Here the mountain breeze begins to blow, the train starts again and very soon, at a turning, a mountain spire is seen. These are the Drus, a soaring pinnacle of stone. The tourists rush to look, then sit down again. The climbers look too, with emotion; for the Drus are always the first peaks that the Montenvers

[1] Now electrified.

train brings into sight. They know them well, and so they wait and look for them as for an old friend.

On the terrace of the Montenvers station, beside the resting engine, the guide is announcing:

"Ladies and gentlemen, in front of you are the Drus, scene of the action of *First on the Rope.* On the left, in profile, is the north face with its Niche, that enormous hollow half-way up. Facing us is the west face with its barrier of overhangs. On the right is the ridge of the Flammes de Pierre...."

The name of Franz Lochmatter[1] will always be associated with this north face. He ventured to attack the wall as early as 1904, with his brother Josef and Captain V.J.E. Ryan. The three climbers managed to ascend to within two hundred and fifty feet of the Niche, a truly remarkable feat for the period. Then in 1930 Felix Batier and Arthur Ravanel climbed the first third of the face; two years later the German climbers Krinner and Kofler fell to their death from a point three hundred

---

[1] Franz Lochmatter of St. Niklaus was universally reckoned the greatest guide of the pre-1914 period. Some of his ascents, such as the south face of the Taschhorn, are still very big undertakings.

feet above the bergschrund. Their comrades Bratschko and Schreiner, who had seen them fall, abandoned their attempt.

A few days later, on 21st and 22nd July 1932, the two Swiss mountaineers, Robert Greloz and André Roch, came up by the ordinary route and made the first and only descent of the face. It must have been an airy, dizzy affair, involving a series of interminable rappels. It was not until 1935 that the three climbers from Geneva, Dupont, Gotch, and Raymond Lambert, succeeded in climbing to a hundred and fifty feet above the Niche, but they could get no further. Three days later, on 31st July and 1st August, the French climber Pierre Allain succeeded in leading the first ascent of the north face of the Drus.

———

A guide spends all his days on the mountains, with different companions. It had been fine for a fortnight and I had been climbing non-stop. But as we descended the Aiguilles du Diable in the afternoon, the sun slowly dissolved in a confusion of clouds streaking the west. My companion, Michel de Campo, was almost happy at the prospect of bad weather; for his holidays were over and he would feel less regret at leaving Chamonix. I was thinking of René Mallieux: I was supposed to be going to bivouac with him at the foot of the north face on the following day, then do the climb the day after, 14th August. Not a day later, for the 15th is the guides' festival and I must be there without fail. Be the weather fair or foul, the Mont Blanc chain is deserted on that day, for the guides of Chamonix and Courmayeur are in their own valleys to celebrate their day. It is the rule and the tradition.

That evening I met René in the Place de la Poste. As usual we wandered round Chamonix doing the tour of the barometers. But in every mountain centre these scientific gadgets are always suspect for promising clear skies even when the west wind is bringing its cloud battalions. Next day it was raining, and René was thoroughly depressed; I knew very well of his long-standing ambition to climb this face. However, in the afternoon there was a clearing and the sun shone weakly; you could even see the tops, and luckily it had not snowed high up. We felt sorry that we had not left after all, but soon the sky clouded over again, and this time the glass really did drop. We wandered disconsolate from cake-shop to cake-shop, from the Guides' Office to the café opposite. I had an idea which would keep coming back, though I dare not put it into words. Finally, however, I asked René:

"Are you in good form? Could you climb fast?"

"Very fast, if necessary." He hesitated for a moment, then added:

"Why?"

"There's one possible solution. If it's fine to-morrow, let's take the first train to the Montenvers, at half past eight, and try to do the climb in the afternoon."

There are moments in life of pure joy, and this was one of them. I could see René's face break into a grin, and knew that the climb was as good as begun. We were so happy that we refused to be damped by the leaden evening sky.

"Quarter past eight at the station then, to-morrow." And we said goodnight. I went to dine with Michel, and later some friends took me to the Outa, to help celebrate their departure. At two in the morning, when we came out, a few stars were winking. By the time my alarm went at seven-thirty it was really fine. René would certainly be at the train! Quickly I got my sack ready, jumped on my bicycle and swept down to the station, where I found him waiting, gleeful and impatient. I breakfasted on the train, reading a newspaper lent me by a tourist; it was hard to believe that we were really going to climb the north face of the Drus. Then, at a turning after Caillet, they appeared before us, even more beautiful than usual. We almost felt they belonged to us.

At a quarter past nine we were at the Montenvers, where the guide was beginning his rigmarole; below, the spivs were waiting to waylay the tourists. But we hurried past and crossed the Mer de Glace. At half past twelve we were picnicking on the last grassy terraces below the face, and three-quarters of an hour later we roped up to cross the bergschrund. Here was the beginning of the climb we had longed for.

Nature is ruled by tradition. Look at the turn of the seasons, the alternation of night and day, of sun and storm. Mountaineering has its traditions too: the slow awakening, the glance at the sky through the hut window, the breakfast swallowed without appetite, the setting out by lantern light, the sunrise, the thousand and one little incidents of the climb, the return to the hut at midday, the lazing about on the terrace. To-day, on the contrary, at the hour when ordinary rational people were drinking their coffee after lunch and when mountaineers had finished their climbs, here were we just beginning. I could not help feeling uneasiness, a sort of dread like that which must have afflicted men in the ages when mountains were the abode only of demons and dragons.

However, with the fine weather back like a gift from heaven, there was nothing for it but to embrace it with open arms; here we were, in shirt-sleeves, at a most unorthodox hour, on the north face of the Drus. It really was fine that August afternoon. The face was in the shade, but the soft air around seemed redolent with gaiety in the place of the cold and severity of the early hours. There was a strange charm here, as if the mountain were about to give up its secrets, on this afternoon bright with all the beauty of autumn.

We had to climb fast, in fact very fast indeed, if I was to attend the guides' festival at Chamonix the next morning. This fact added zest to the whole day. To go fast merely for the sake of going fast usually seems senseless, but on this occasion it was quite different; we *had* only these few hours to climb the two thousand five hundred feet of this face. But René had not exaggerated when he said that he was a quick mover; he kept on my heels the whole time. At about 3 P.M. we arrived at the Niche, printed like a giant's thumb-mark in the clay of our mountain. We stopped to look at it, and also at the west face which soared like a stone waterspout from the moraine direct to the sky.

"In ten years' time that will be climbed," I said to René.[1]

We ate a few dates, some currants and an orange—fruits of the sun in the chill north face—and went on. We found ourselves climbing with ease and pleasure. Our movements were linked in smooth rhythm, like water flowing from a spring. All skills have this effect on a well-trained body: they remove the sense of difficulty and leave only the pleasure of a task prepared and well performed. As children we used to climb trees, and per-

---

[1] The first ascent of the west face was made in 1952 by Guido Magnone, L. Berardini, M. Laine and A. Dagory.

haps that instinct was with us still. If we had been suddenly stopped and asked the question "Why do you climb mountains?" I feel sure that we would have answered on that day: "That's what we are made for." We have the instinct for it, the love of rocks and the necessary skill, so that we can climb without being worried by the technical problems. Thus the whole climb was pure joy, for, while superficially watching over the actual ascent, the spirit had leisure to wander happily. It was an exquisite afternoon; no incident marred the day.

The breeze that fanned us was cool and gentle. The sun, hidden behind the west face, spared us the overpowering heat of its direct rays, but we were cheered by its nearness. Down below, the Montenvers train continued to rattle along, the torrent to run its course, the waterfall to break over the jagged cliff edge. Close at hand the rock had a good rocky smell, its roughness bit firmly into our rubber soles and our finger-tips. It was all very nice and very reassuring, like the shade of an oak-tree; we felt as if the world was made for us, this corner of the planet on which we knew peace.

I climbed first, because of my position as guide, but

René's job was as vital as mine. Almost the whole time we climbed together, without stopping, both in order to go faster and because we each had confidence in the other. It was now six months since I had gone to Brussels to give a lecture to the Belgian Alpine Club at the invitation of René Mallieux, its vice-president. It was then that I learned of this old passion of his—the north face of the Drus. He is older than I, and had been in Chamonix in 1935, the year of the first ascent. The idea of climbing it was born then, but the war intervened and he had to put it aside. On that visit the previous winter I fanned the smouldering flame. The moments when happiness and friendship are created are simple and unpretentious; they are so woven into the natural course of things that we hardly notice them.

Now at last we were on the face together, and as we climbed I became aware of a special source of happiness. I could not define it; at first it seemed to come from the climb, and yet the song which rose to my lips had surely some other origin. True, there were tinglings of the atmosphere and the earth around us, the taste of air and the gold of sunshine on our mountain; but all that could be no more than a fragrance. The real truth was that we were two men in a realm of rock, both climbing towards the same star. René's pleasure lay in bringing off a nine-year-old plan, mine in helping him to do so. I felt happy to be on the Drus, but my happiness, here as elsewhere, lay in my task of leading a companion. For where would a guide be without his companion? Whatever the weather, no matter what the climbing difficulties, my need was to play the same tune as he, for that is the best gift that our mountains can give us. One man of the two, as he climbs to the summit, is doing his job. The other is on holiday; and the cream of their combined effort is friendship.

At last we were sitting side by side on a granite terrace. It was snowing slightly, and darkness had fallen. While we had been finishing the climb the storm had broken. We passed under the summit along the quartz ledge to rejoin the ordinary route and begin the descent. But after two rappels we were forced to put on our bivouac hoods and stop for the night. The snow interfered with our plans, but was not in itself unpleasant.

Rain is disagreeable, but snow is as much part of the mountain as are sunshine and clear skies. In this case the clouds cannot have been very thick, nor was it altogether dark. We were bathed in a faintly luminous glimmer; for behind the clouds, as we well knew, the full moon was shining.

At about ten o'clock it grew cold. The banks of cloud dissolved like the sheets of mist above rivers that disappear under the morning sun; they drew away over the Valley of Chamonix, separating us from the world of men. The yellow moon appeared in a black sky; under its beams the fresh snow sparkled like stardust. Now it was very cold, and as we crouched side by side in our down jackets we were cradled in the earth's very bones. The beauty of heaven's vault was in our hearts, and with our eyes we followed the path of the numberless stars. Then a light breeze arose. We thought of the first men to climb the mountains. Nearly six thousand feet below us, beside the glacier, the little lakes of Tacul shone like precious stones. On our right, in the valley, Chamonix lay sleeping under a sea of cloud that shifted with the wind....

——

When we arrived back in the valley next morning the ceremony at the cemetery and the Blessing of the Ice-Axes had already taken place. That meant that I would be fined for being late.

In the afternoon I climbed on the Gaillands in the demonstration which is part of the guides' festival.

THE MATTERHORN

The Matterhorn is the most startling of mountains, a mountain ruled in geometric upward lines. It is the ideal peak, such as children imagine before they have ever seen a summit at all. Born as I was by the sea, it is what I pictured when I heard the word "mountain": a pyramid surrounded by glaciers and pointing to the sky. But this pyramid is the more beautiful in that it stands alone. All around lie nothing but mountain ruins: peaks that have fallen asleep, bent over and crumpled.

When, after the first ascent of Mont Blanc in 1786, almost all the summits were climbed, the Matterhorn remained still inaccessible. This was the great age of Alpine mountaineering. Many climbers looked with passionate desire at this peak. Some made attempts; but all failed.

Two men refused to look on their failures as more than temporary set-backs to eventual success: Edward Whymper, the Englishman, burning with a fierce determination, and Jean-Antoine Carrel, of Valdot, who loved the mountain in whose shadow he had been born. Sometimes these two joined forces, but at heart each was too ambitious for victory to be willing to share it. On 14th July 1865 came the climax. Whymper got there first, reaching the summit by the Swiss ridge. But, as is well known, his great victory was followed by a tragic disaster. On the descent four of his party of seven fell to their death down the north face. Two days later Carrel reached the summit by the Italian ridge.

The battle so worthily begun was to continue on the two other ridges and on the four faces. Of these the north face is the finest. It is contained by the Hörnli and Zmutt ridges, and seen from the Zinal Rothorn it has the simplicity of a perfect triangle. In profile it appears as a giant torso of rock, 3,600 feet high. It looks difficult, but more than that it is dangerous. The rock is bad, the ice glassy. There are no halting places, no shelter at all in case of storm. But worst of all are the rock-falls, against which no skill, however great, can prevail. Only a few days in each year do they cease sweeping the wall, so you must be on the spot at the time. But it is not easy to judge the moment, for the whims of the Matterhorn are inscrutable.

Among all the great north faces of the Alps that of the Matterhorn was the first to be seriously attempted, and it was the first climbed. The lowest section is steep, the middle third comes near to the vertical, the upper part lies back a little and yet remains exposed. The key to the climb seems to be the couloir which cuts the middle section, but which, for that very reason, forms a natural channel for avalanches.

In August 1923 two Austrians, Horeschowsky and Piekelko, climbed the very steep ice slope at the foot of the wall, crossed the rocks to the left of the couloir, and came out at 13,000 feet on the Hörnli ridge, near the Solvay hut. Then in September 1928 two guides from Täsch, Victor Imboden and Kaspar Mooser, reached a point 1,650 feet above the bergschrund, to the right of the couloir. Caught by nightfall, they bivouacked and only got down with difficulty. There followed many other attempts, until early August 1931, when the amazing news went round the Zermatt valley that the north face of the Matterhorn had been climbed by two lads from Munich, the brothers Franz and Toni Schmid.

In the early hours of 31st July they passed the bergschrund and attacked the ice slope. Then, profiting by a lucky day when stones were not falling, they climbed the couloir and bivouacked at 13,600 feet. The next day, 1st August, they reached the summit at about two o'clock in the afternoon, in a raging storm, having remained clinging to the face for thirty-three hours. Since that memorable day the north face had been climbed no more than three or four times, and never by a French party. But for us this was only a secondary consideration; the real truth was that the Matterhorn had cast its spell over us.

—

Raymond Simond lived in one of the loveliest spots in the high valley of the Arve: above the plain of Les Tines, opposite the forest. He was not a guide, but a hotel-keeper. He loved mountaineering, and despite a job which kept him busy in the tourist season, it was not rare to meet him on a summit. But the chief reason why I enjoyed his company was that he had a wide love of all mountain things. Certainly he climbed, but he also went crystal hunting. He had done the Aiguille Verte[1] by the Nant-Blanc, but he also visited the Lac Blanc and the Aiguilles Rouges. He loved the smell of freshly cut wood in the autumn, he knew all about mushrooms and flowers, and he loved the forest.

The year before, on one of those autumn days which are a last gift from heaven, we climbed together the south ridge of the Aiguille Noire de Peuterey[2]. Now, during these first summer days, we were dreaming of the north face of the Matterhorn. Like myself, Raymond loved the distant mountains. They are more attractive in that they lie beyond our daily horizon. So it happened that on 26th June 1946 we left Chamonix for Zermatt.

On the way I thought of a postcard received one day from Max Chamson: "Returned from this wonderful heap of rubble." On the back of the card was a photograph of the Matterhorn. To-day it seemed to me that I understood better the meaning of those words "wonder-

---

[1] 13,541 feet high: satellites of this peak are the greater and lesser Dru.

[2] On the south side of Mont Blanc, 12,380 feet high.

ful heap of rubble." The main interest of a mountaineer lies in the business of climbing; often he is rewarded by a very fine ascent. But in climbing for climbing's sake he tends to care little which peak he is scaling. For Raymond and myself the Matterhorn had aroused anew the pleasure of choice, the direct, unreasoned attraction of a mountain, which gives to the whole ascent the feeling of a pilgrimage. For the climbing here is not always interesting, and the rock is bad. Cables desecrate the Matterhorn's ridges, the ascent is long and in some places irksome. But all that was of little consequence, for the mountain itself had captivated us.

It was my first visit to Zermatt, indeed to the Valais. Raymond had been there already, and had done the Furggen ridge. I myself had never really seen the Matterhorn except in photographs. From Mont Blanc or the Oberland I had just glimpsed it in the distance. And now, while the little train jolted us up amongst the anonymous crowd, I had arrived at the moment in the pilgrimage when you are "going to see." You are always afraid of being disappointed. Suppose it were not true? Suppose it were not all that I expected? Truth often brings disillusion.

Yet in this case the truth is that here is the perfect mountain. Think of 1865, then of the fascinating story of the mountain's conquest and exploration: Penhall, Mummery, Guido Rey, the brothers Schmid on their bicycles...[1] No, it *cannot* be disappointing. And as you approach you come under its spell. The zigzags leading to the Schwarzsee are long and tedious, yet gradually the great history of the towering peak grips you. Can it be that you yourself will have a place in the epic? You imagine Whymper, Carrel and the rest roaming round the mountain. We are their heirs, and this "heap of rubble" lives as much by the right of the men who have loved it as of its own cold beauty. I began to understand what urges us towards the great climbs and the last unsolved problems. It is the desire to be worthy of our heritage, not to content ourselves with treading in the footsteps of the pioneers.

At one in the morning we passed silently along below the séracs which protect the north face. Then, finding a weakness, we made our way between the blocks of ice. It was very cold. At dawn we were passing the traditional bergschrund. Above it we mounted quickly on cram-

---

[1] Pioneers of various routes up the Matterhorn.

pons up the great slope. Below, the snow had been as hard as you could wish; but higher it became horrible: powdery, above a lower layer of ice. We had chosen the beginning of the season in order to avoid stone-falls and to have the mountain to ourselves. But it was in very bad condition. Above the ice slope we traversed right in the direction of the couloir, which is the key to the middle section of the north face. But on reaching it we considered it too dangerous, so we crossed it quickly and tried to climb the wall which separates it from the Zmutt ridge. It is a very steep wall, harder than the couloir but also less dangerous. Soon after we had started up it a rock avalanche, which we heard but could not see properly, crashed down the couloir and sent a cloud of mingled rock and snow billowing upwards.

The wall is not vertical, like a limestone cliff, but it is just as exposed. Never a ledge! Always those illusory little platforms which recede as you approach them! On this enormous face there is not a single definite pitch; everything is exactly like everything else. There is no "geometrical" climbing as in the chain of Mont Blanc. The whole time you must be dodging to and fro. Apart from a few major lines—the Zmutt ridge on the right, the couloir on the left, the shoulder above—there is nothing that stands out. You cannot say: "We have just climbed the 'Standard Five crack' or 'the seventy-five-metre corner.' " There *is* no "Standard Five crack" to be found or climbed; there *is* no "seventy-five-metre corner," no characteristic slab, no second or sixth degree chimney. We simply wandered here and there, choosing the best line, over this vast and dizzy slope. Here we could not triumph over some great difficulty, as in the ascent of the Grey Tower of the Grandes Jorasses, or the barrier of overhangs on the Piz Badile. We just went on with our unexciting and patient work. Yet we were gripped by a strange charm, by the giddy pleasure of being lost in a mass of ice-glued stones. The game consists in entering voluntarily into the prison of the Matterhorn's north face, and then escaping. And the interest lies in finding the escape route. For there is no security in these vertical, crumbling slabs held in place by the frost, shining with verglas, linked together by sheets of black ice under a fair mask of powder snow. We fixed no pitons, for they are not easy to hammer in and do not stay firm. The most that I ever fixed was two, one a traverse, and Raymond, as he followed, pulled them out with a tug of the hand. And from time to time the Matterhorn crumbled a little more. Rocks fell whistling into the depths.

Seen from a distance the Matterhorn looks unbreakable: a solid, sober pyramid. It is as if the winds, rather than wear it down or tip it over, act as a knife to sharpen it. But as you climb you cannot understand how this heap of stones soldered by ice can remain so upright. Nothing holds. Immense flakes are laid one on the other like crazy piles of plates. Everything seems to be in suspense: a suspense in the very act of living. And yet— what sacrilege to imagine the Matterhorn beheaded, worn, rounded like its neighbours! Instead, climbing this enchanted summit, this fragment of earth that soars near to heaven, one can easily credit these stones with magical powers: with the power of never growing old a lasting proof of the urge of our living planet towards the magnet of the skies.

We climbed with crampons, which we were to keep on throughout the ascent, since the face was thickly covered with snow. The effort was unremitting, if nowhere extreme. Never a quarter of an hour's respite, never five minutes, never one single moment. Always these slabs, cracked and crumbling, broken and blasted, glued with ice and glazed with verglas. Always these glassy boiler-plates, couloirs and icicles draped in spotless snow; always these piles of rock leaves balanced one upon the other. Miracle of equilibrium! Never must you pull upon a hold, or it will come out like a drawer and upset the balance of the whole structure. Raymond had long since broken one of the forepoints of his left crampon, but he carried on as if nothing had happened. He was the ideal companion, always cheerful, always in his element in this environment of high mountains.

The approach to the summit was a pleasant one. We sensed the two ridges, Zmutt and Hörnli, closing in on us. At nine in the evening we stepped out on to the final crest: a fine finish to the day. Alone up here we had the benefit of the sun's last light. Down there our fellow men were already in darkness, and a line of lights picked out the main street of Zermatt. At our feet the great slope dropped sharply away. The north face! What disagreeable climbing, and yet what a splendid climb!

We stood upon this most wonderful of mountains and looked around. Fragile creatures set upon a pyramid that soars to heaven, we were witnesses of earth's bedtime hour. Then we too plunged down into the night.

THE CIMA GRANDE
DI LAVAREDO

Erosion has sculpted the Dolomites. But they look as if they had thrust their way out of the earth's crust. They provide a violent, fantastic contrast with their surroundings; for these petrified organ pipes seem to be born direct from the magical woods, since there is no intermediate glacier and very little eternal snow. The climate is too warm, and in any case the walls are too steep for snow to rest on them. People often compare the Dolomites with the Western Alps. You might just as well compare gentians with edelweiss, for mountains too are as the earth gave them to us. Each massif has its own form and colour, each rock its own texture and smell. The pleasures that mountains give us vary each day, and it is for us to understand them, not try to limit them. Don't go to the Matterhorn, for instance, in the hope of having an interesting rock-climb. The charm of the Matterhorn lies elsewhere, in its history and its form. In the Dolomites it is almost always pointless to carry an ice-axe. Better here to come to terms with the terrifying void which will be your closest companion on the ascent of wall or pinnacle. In other districts the walls are abrupt and sometimes very steep. Here they are quite geometrically vertical; and some of them, also geometrically, overhanging.

What then of the climber, face to face with such walls? Man is the same the world over, as sensitive to the charm of the woods below as to the challenge of the great face, whether it be of spotless ice or red rock. "Where there's a will there's a way" is as true at Cortina d'Ampezzo[1] as at Chamonix, at Bolzano[1] as at Courmayeur. The climbers of the Dolomites wear velvet trousers, at Zermatt breeches are of thick cloth. But the human stuff inside is the same.

The Dolomites need the warmth of the sun, without which they would be insipid, dull and lifeless, sometimes

[1] The great centres for climbers in the Dolomites.

a dirty grey, sometimes faded yellow. But one ray of sunshine is enough to give them life; the effect of kindly warmth is to make them shimmer, take on colour and charm for all their verticality. In this riot of light only the north faces remain aloof. A faintly lighter tint just covers them, a reflection from the brightness around, but apart from that they remain unbending, maintaining an impressive dignity in their isolation. Among these mountains the north face of the Cima Grande di Lavaredo is one of the most noble and the most typical. Some are higher or harder. But whether it be its name, its history, or the personalities of the first party to climb it, this is the most coveted and the most climbed of all.

An important part of the pleasure of Alpine climbing lies in the discovery of new ground. That is why mountaineers dream of the Himalaya. It is also why I have always wanted to explore new ranges, to do climbs far away from Chamonix, which is my home every summer. And for a long time the Dolomites fascinated me.

At the beginning of July 1948, then, my wife, Jean Deudon and myself set out for this land of light, only to find, as everywhere else that year, nothing but rain. The rocks looked as dismal as a tomb. Between two showers

we climbed the Sella Towers; then, according to pro-
gramme, we made for the Cima Grande. We wanted to
see it as much as to climb it, and we profited by a clearing at the end of one afternoon to go up to the Longères
hut. It was deserted, dark and gloomy, with not a soul
about but the custodian and some servants. While we
were eating the *minestra* (vegetable soup) a fine rain
began to fall again, steadily: a monotonous beat to which
we had become accustomed. But suddenly loud crashes
summoned us outside. From the wall of the Cima
Grande great blocks as large as the towers of Notre
Dame were detaching themselves, rolling, rebounding,
bursting, belabouring the scree and drawing in their
wake a wave of smaller boulders which continued to
slide down the slope to the very bottom of the valley. It
was very dark: no sky, no stars, not even the summit of
the Cima Grande visible; heavy, swollen clouds dragged
wearily across the face of our earth. And what a din, despite the humid atmosphere, which absorbed some of
the noise! Assuredly the Tre Cime di Lavaredo were not
on their best behaviour. I confess that I have never since
seen a stone avalanche of such size; it was certainly not
typical of the "mountains of light."

Next day the weather looked a little better. At least it was not raining any more. "Let's go and see," said Jean. Little by little, under a feeble sun, the Tre Cime came to life again. At the Forcella we stopped in amazement. Seen in profile, as we looked along the line of them, the north faces astounded us, with their overhangs and lines of dizzy slabs. We pushed on into this sanctuary of soaring summits and dead, fallen stone. After the night's rain the water which had seeped in through the limestone now oozed out along the great slabs, which seemed to be bleeding a grey-black blood. Even in fine weather climbing would be out of the question; but to remove any lingering regrets the rain started again. The summer of 1948 was bad indeed.

The Cima Grande, and more especially its north face, would not be so beautiful or so striking if it were not a part of the trinity of the Tre Cime; it would lose a lot if it stood alone. Any one summit, even the Cima Grande itself, would be nothing but a huge block, mighty and melancholy, such as one can find elsewhere.

The key to the north face of the Tre Cime di Lavaredo lies in its simple lines. From the horizontal of the scree slopes there spring the vertical northern flanks. They make a sharp contrast; as if in fashioning them some giant had had at his disposal a huge block of shapeless stone, and with one masterly stroke of the axe had cut out the north side in a strictly straight line; then, finding his handiwork still too massive, had carved two deep gaps with two extra little blows, thus giving us three summits that vie with each other for elegance and purity of form. The stone shavings have filled up the top end of the Val Rimbon and formed the Pian da Rin. Thus they give the horizontal line to set off the uprightness of the walls. There, on the ground, is the débris; there, above our heads, the living mountain. Can we doubt that the ocean and Father Time have joined forces to provide for the greater pleasure and happiness of climbers?

For a long time the north face of the Cima Grande remained the unsolved problem of the Dolomites, and the date of its conquest coincides with the "north-face" era, which began in 1931 with the Matterhorn and ended in 1938 with the Walker Spur and the Eigerwand. One name above all others clings to this north face of the Cima Grande: that of Emilio Comici. A native of Trieste and a mountaineer "by adoption," he was the first man to believe it could be climbed. Small and agile, muscular and yet a dreamer, a romantic even, he was one of the greatest climbers of the Dolomites. To his name must be joined that of the brothers Dimai of Cortina. The height of the Cima Grande is no more than 9,836 feet, and of its north face no more than 1,800 feet. But the first 720 feet are definitely overhanging, and the rest is vertical. You may well wonder if it is possible to climb a slab which literally overhangs over the whole of its 720 feet. Determination is not enough, for a technique was also needed to overcome this type of problem.

By dint of hammering in an almost continuous series of pitons, planting them with infinite pains and trusting them completely, success came at last. On 13th and 14th August 1933 Comici and the brothers Dimai managed to reach the top of this formidable wall. Once resolved, this problem was to become the master key to the conquest of other faces. But while losing its mystery, the Cima Grande continued to exercise its charm, a charm heightened rather than diminished by the first ascent. Even now it is the most sought after of all the great faces, the most climbed both by romantically enthusiastic youth and by seasoned mountaineers. They come to find an atmosphere which is not only moving but out of this world. They come as to a sort of consecration. And I too was a pilgrim like the rest. For I had long succumbed to the fascination, and my expedition with Jean Deudon had only increased my desire.

Here I was then at the end of the 1949 season, climbing to the Longères hut once more, this time to join Gino Soldà. He is one of the best climbers in the Dolomites, but first and foremost he is an exceptionally nice person. He reminded me of Henri Moulin, my companion on my first climb in the Barre des Ecrins: a strong man and also a fine character. He was then forty years old, with solid experience as a guide, but he still had the enthusiasm of a boy. He had successfully climbed all the hardest routes in the Dolomites; and this, which for others would be a feat indeed, he took as a matter of course. His extraordinary strength and resolution allowed him to do these things without apparent effort. But his foremost qualities seemed to me to be his gaiety and sincerity.

Soldà introduced me to two friends: Mazzetta, a young guide from Auronzo, and Roland Stern, an Austrian student. Both of these would accompany us the next day on the north face of the Grande. Together we passed an evening which I shall always remember. First we went for a walk to the Tre Cime hut, to have one more look at the great wall and to walk for the pure pleasure of walking among the mountains. Besides this there was a pleasantly truant air about the whole party. Soldà is a guide like myself. We find our job the finest in the world; but to-day we were away from it. We walked and jumped about with not a care or responsibility in the world. To-morrow we would be climbing like schoolboys. We felt ourselves back at just twenty years old. And now, at the Longères hut again, we watched the night slowly descend.

The last hours of daylight are very moving in the Dolomites. The sun plays out his terrible game with the great stone façades. The rock, which is only alive in his light, passes through an assortment of fleeting colours, each one of which you long to capture, while the sun bids farewell, falls down and finally disappears below the trap-door which is the horizon. Then silence spreads over the deserted cliffs, then a sense of mystery as you listen to the familiar noises of the earth, the murmur of insects, the cow-bells, the light breeze. The lights of Auronzo and Misurine wink back with a confidential air at the stars ranged across the sky. Then comes the cold.

Men do not speak, they rather feel the brotherhood born of a common love of the mountains. Back in the warm hut, over our evening meal, Soldà filled us with his own gaiety.

At half past seven the next morning we were at the foot of the face. Though we had purposely started late it was too early, for the limestone cliffs of the Cima Grande were still as cold as the marble top of a café table. It was 14th September, and now the sun rose too far to the south for even the most oblique ray to warm the face, however slightly. The night had been cool, and higher up, in the chimney, we would find ice.

It was with some emotion that I found myself roping up to Soldà, then watching him begin to climb. He had already climbed the north face once with Gervasutti, and I counted myself lucky indeed to be with him to-day. For I always think the companion with whom I am roped as important as the climb that we do together. From the start we sensed the character of the route; a traverse to the left led straight into space, with the wall curving away below our feet. There was no need now to turn round to see the scree. There it was between our legs. And what a treat to watch Soldà climbing! He seemed not to cling to the rock but to skim it, scarcely touching it with the tips of his fingers and toes. What style! He reminded me of James Couttet[1] skiing down in some big competition. You see him pass, perfectly upright and assured on his skis, controlled in movement and never out of balance. You say to yourself: "He's not moving at all!" You look at your watch and find that James has saved a whole second.

Up above, Soldà was already at the stance. "Come on!" he called down. When I was watching him climbing it had seemed simple. I tried to do as he did, but I was not accustomed to this rock, or to this sense of space. It is highly impressive! And there was another habit which I had not acquired: that of climbing second rather than leading. I found the rope in front of me a hindrance rather than a help.

But as I rose my uneasiness disappeared. Indeed I became imbued with a feeling of joy such as I had never known before, a joy such as no granite walls can ever give. Steep they may be, but they are not vertical for hundreds of feet. And this joy sprang mainly from the foundation of the wall that we were climbing. Apart

[1] A former world skiing champion.

from its beauty and its history, the charm of the north face of the Cima Grande lies in its uniform smoothness as far as the eye can see, without hollow or hump, not merely overhanging in places, but throughout. Civetta, Marmolada, Sassolungo, Brenta Alta—all the other north faces are furrowed with chimneys and couloirs, furnished with ridges and spurs, whereas the north face of the Cima Grande is as uninterrupted as a calm sea. Above, below, to the right and to the left, the eye wanders and is lost. And if you drop a stone it falls straight to the scree with not a bounce nor a ricochet, beside the wall arched like the inside of a cathedral dome.

When Gino reached the end of his rope it was my turn to climb, and when I had rejoined him he went ahead again. Below us Mazzetta and Stern repeated the same manoeuvre. There we were, four men of three different nationalities, united in a world of stone by a single passion. But what a curious language we talked to each other—almost the language of the deaf and dumb!

The rock was not always perfect: loose limestone running very much in strata, fairly friable and breaking off like lumps of sugar. The resting-places were no more than minute ledges on which you placed the front half of the feet to stand upright. Only one was luxurious, a flake half unstuck from the wall on which it was possible to sit, with feet hanging over space. The route is strewn with pitons; indeed there are far too many, and Soldà only used those that were necessary. That is the fate of artificial climbs, whether here or on the Piz Badile and other peaks of the Eastern Alps. It is also the reason why, from being extremely severe at the time of their first ascent, they become little by little a sort of rope-ladder, their merit decreasing far more quickly than that of routes on higher mountains, such as the north face of the Matterhorn.

The Chamonix guides are accustomed to putting their feet on ice. One might well say, watching Soldà and Mazzetta climb, that the Dolomite guides are accustomed to stepping on space. Throughout the day nothing untoward occurred, no storm, no fall, no accident of any sort; nothing except the revelation of how men can dance out a fantastic ballet on a slice of vertical rock. What is more they can feel at home there, for this is their element.

As we climbed higher I found that the terrifying void was no longer a weight on my legs, dragging me down, but a pleasant companion. The distant scree slope framed between my feet became a part of my intimate environment. My initial fears had quite left me, and I felt as if I had thrown off a heavy burden. Gino too was content, and from time to time he burst into song as he climbed. If only he knew how happy I was to be here! When I had asked him several months before at Vicenza "How is it possible to climb a continuously overhanging wall for 720 feet?" he had replied: "You'll see." And now that we had reached the top of the yellow slabs he said to me amusedly:

"If you drop a stone, not only will it not hit the wall, it will bounce on the scree slope more than sixty feet away from the bottom of the face."

And it was quite true, for I tried it! I was surprised that it should not for one second occur to him to think: "If we fall, we'll do the same as the stone." He knew as much, but such a morbid idea did not even enter his head. That is why I enjoyed being with him, for we were not daredevils or madcaps. We did not like being afraid, we loved life as we loved our job.

Above here the angle of the wall changes; from being overhanging it becomes vertical. I took the lead as far as the level of the long traverse, where Gino took over again to allow me to photograph; he continued in the lead to the top, where we found the sun once more. The whole climb had an end-of-the-season air, for the autumn was near. Once again Gino was bubbling over with his infectious gaiety. Off with the rope, and down the ordinary route we went at a run. For to-day there was no need to bivouac. This time the stars were in our hearts, not in the sky.

The North Face of
the Eiger

The Eiger's north wall springs in one startling sweep from the pleasant meadows around the Little Scheidegg. It is black, cold and joyless. There is no glacier, no eternal snow to separate it from the rest of the world; it stands up like a pyramid in a field of flowers. It is always in the shade, seeming to receive no benefit from the great daily voyage of the earth round the sun. Only a few rare shafts touch its crest and give it a semblance of warmth. There its bulk looms above the pastoral landscape.

The face is 5,250 feet high, hollowed like a sick man's chest, often veiled in mist or blotted out by clouds; life up there is strangely remote from that of the flowers and animals at its feet. It stands aloof, unbeautiful, inspiring fear. In structure it is not simple, being made up of compact slabs and tortuous chimneys worn by the ice. At its feet lies an immense débris of scree. Then a short wall of rock girdles it, supporting a gigantic, crumbled coping that rises to 9,200 feet. This is the lower third of the face. The middle third comprises the three ice slopes. The upper third rises as vertically as a wall in the Dolomites to the summit crest.

From time to time the immense wall cracks under the torturing hand of frost. Then mighty avalanches rumble down its couloir. That is the trumpet note of the Eiger, answering the pastoral chants of the shepherds' horns at Alpiglen below. Black stone and glassy ice, alone, unloved, the Eiger is slowly breaking to pieces. Yet for its conquest men have given their lives.

The attempts began in 1935. Peters and Meier had just climbed the central spur of the Grandes Jorasses; German and Austrian climbers now turned their attention to the Eiger face. Two Munich climbers, Mehringer and Sedlmeier, made an attempt on 22nd August. Four days later they were seen for the last time, climbing the third snow patch. Then the weather broke, and the mountain was enveloped in storm. The rescue parties were unable to set out, and when conditions improved, the wall was so plastered in snow that nothing was to be seen of the climbers. Some days later a pilot flew close to the face and at last picked out one figure stiff and upright against the rock. His companion had fallen; the body remained till the following winter before it was carried down by an avalanche.

In 1936 a number of German parties were prowling around the foot of the face, but the weather was bad and most of them gave up. Four young climbers, however, persisted: two Germans, Hinterstoisser and Kurz, and two Austrians, Angerer and Rainer. These joined forces and began their attempt on 18th July. By a clever piece of climbing Hinterstoisser overcame the key passage to the lower part of the face. This was a diagonal traverse[1] which, however, was later to prove his undoing. On the second day mist hid the wall. On the morning of the third there was a clearing, but they hesitated to continue; one of them had been injured on the head, the weather was overcast, and the day before they had suc-

[1] It is now called the Hinterstoisser traverse.

ceeded in climbing only some six hundred feet. They reached the spot where Sedlmeier and Mehringer had died and there, too late, they decided to retreat. They descended so slowly that they were again overtaken by night, and had their third bivouac in miserable conditions. On the morning of the fourth day they reached the key passage, but were unable to climb in the opposite direction down the famous traverse, which had in fact become a trap.

Meanwhile guides had set out to their rescue. Adolph and Christian Rubi, Glatthard and Schlunegger started from the Eigerwand station of the rack-railway which pierces the mountain and comes out at the Jungfraujoch.[1] They then traversed horizontally left towards the climbers. Despite the very bad conditions they arrived within three hundred feet of Kurz, who told them of the death of his companions. Hinterstoisser had fallen, Angerer was frozen to death, while Rainer hung below, strangled by the rope.

The night passed without the guides being able to reach Kurz, who thus endured a terrible fourth night

---

[1] A glass window set in the front allows tourists on the railway to look down and across the face.

out. At dawn of the fifth day they resumed rescue operations. They reached a point only one hundred and twenty feet below Kurz and shouted instructions. "Cut the rope attached to Rainer!" With great difficulty he succeeded, and the body fell away. "Now pull on the rope. Separate the strands." Kurz pulled up the rope, undid the frozen knots and separated the three strands, stiff though they were. "Tie the three strands together." Thus the new thread, three times as long as the old, reached the guides, who were able to send up food and other assistance. Because of the terrible conditions, with the mountain covered in fresh snow, all this took a very long time. Yet Kurz had still the strength to bring everything up and put on his rappel rope. After hours of effort he at last began the descent. But suddenly a knot in the rope jammed in the snap-ring to which his rappel was attached. The guides shouted encouragement. Then a small avalanche smothered rescuers and rescued, and the wind blew Kurz out from the wall, just as Glatthard, climbing on Rubi's shoulders, almost succeeded in touching him. He moaned several times, and died.

In 1937 the attempts started again, still led by Austrians and Germans. The most important of these was carried out by Rebitsch and Vorg. After two days' climbing they reached the place where Sedlmeier and Mehringer had died. Then the dawn of the third day confirmed their suspicions of the evening before: bad weather had set in. They turned back; after a hundred and twelve hours on the face they were the first to come down alive from the higher ice slopes.

The year of the successful ascent, 1938, was marked by yet another tragedy. Two Italians, Sandri and Menti, made their attempt at the beginning of the season and were lost in a storm. In July, however, various parties of Germans and Austrians were vying with one another at the foot of the face. On the 20th two Munich climbers, Heckmair and Vorg, started up. They bivouacked above the second rock bastion. On the next day, just as they had decided to turn back, two Austrians, Kasparek and Harrer[1], appeared, followed by two more, Fraisl and Brandovsky. The weather was uncertain, but the four Austrians continued while the two Germans gave up. At the end of the day Fraisl and Brandovsky came down in their turn, encouraging Heckmair and Vorg to make a

---

[1] Author of *Seven Years in Tibet* (Rupert Hart-Davies, 1953).

further attempt. They launched their attack in the early dawn of the 21st, and profiting by the tracks of the Austrians, they caught them up at about eleven o'clock. After a short pause they joined forces with them, taking over the lead. By 2 P.M. they had reached the top of the ice slopes where Sedlmeier and Mehringer had died, and that evening they established their bivouac in a niche set in the great chimney called the Ramp. Next day the climbing became very difficult, and towards evening the weather deteriorated while they were on the last snow slope framed in the final barrier of rocks, nicknamed "the Spider" because of its shape. Here they were very nearly carried away by avalanches, and soon it grew dark. This meant a third bivouac for the Austrians, a second one for the Germans.

Next day the wall was plastered with snow, but with a ferocious determination they mastered the last difficulties, and at 3:30 P.M. reached the top of the Eiger's north face.

———

At eight o'clock in the evening the little rack-railway from Lauterbrunnen deposited Jean Bruneau, Paul Habran, Pierre Leroux, Guido Magnone, and myself at the Eigergletscher station. In a trice our bulging sacks were cluttering up the empty station restaurant. After supper the guardian accompanied us to the dormitory. At the door he asked:

"What time do you want to be called?"

"Two o'clock."

"You're going for the Eiger north face?" He had guessed, and without waiting for a reply, ignoring the starry sky and the cold, he added:

"That means bad weather, if you're going to the north face. It's a tradition."

But we refused to believe him: we were the same happy party as when we set out, early that morning, from Chamonix. We sorted out our gear and food for the climb, packed it and went to bed.

The nights before our great battles are always strange. There we were, the five of us, and we had been gay. But now, in the silence, each one must have been dreaming of the great wall waiting there, very close to us, huge and indifferent. Would we have better luck now than on our first attempt a fortnight ago? For Leroux and myself had been here already. We had been in excellent form and we knew that for this climb above all others you must move fast. Otherwise the traditional storm will descend suddenly upon you with a violence from which there is no protection. In three hours we had climbed the lower third of the face, including the famous Hinterstoisser traverse, when suddenly the brutal noise of falling stones stopped us in mid course. We looked carefully to see where they came from; they were peeling off from three thousand feet above us, from the summit ridge now warmed by the sun's rays. We waited, in the hope that they might stop; and indeed they did not fall continuously, but at frequent intervals. Once we said to each other:

"Let's go on; other people have succeeded under similar conditions. And what are the chances of our ever coming here again? We're both guides, and booked up."

The temptation to go on was very great. We hesitated, then decided to turn back. We were in the state of mind of a child who sees his favourite toy snatched from him; and yet as we descended we felt a great peace within, the recognition of a virtue other than the mere climbing of a high mountain.

If only the morrow would be cold, so that there were no stone-falls! The mountaineer can try to overcome any difficulty up to the sixth degree; but he has no power against a danger which has nothing to do with his climbing skill.... These thoughts filled my mind that evening and denied sleep. Since that last attempt luck had smiled on us again. Pierrot had done the Walker Spur, Guido the west face of the Drus, Jean was in great form, while Paul and myself had been on the Grandes Jorasses a few days before. The success of these climbs was the reason why we were now five instead of two for the Eiger north face. Five is a large number for such a venture; but climbing is nothing if not an opportunity to cement friendships.

When at last I went to sleep I dreamed happily of the Grandes Jorasses, where a few days before I had led Paul. He told me later that for the first few rope-lengths of the Walker Spur he was very impressed indeed. That was natural, and it increased his enjoyment of the climb. Then little by little doubts disappeared, their place to be taken by a serious but very real happiness. I knew well that the traverse of the ice bands was delicate and airy, that soon afterwards there was suddenly an astonishing view of the 250-foot corner, and that my companion would enjoy it. I said nothing, but each time I waited for his smile. I knew that he was accustomed to the limestone of the Ardennes, where he used to go for training every Sunday; I knew that he liked delicate climbing, and I said to myself: "He'll enjoy those smooth slabs on the Grey Tower." Higher up I said to myself: "Paul has never spent a night out on a great face, but he's too much of a nature-lover not to enjoy that too." Shortly before nightfall we prepared our bivouac at a height of about 13,000 feet. The nip in the air was a promise of good weather. It was very cold, and a great peace reigned over earth and sky. When we awoke the sun was once more gilding the planet; our climb began again with the ecstasy of a hymn to life. I felt very happy, as if the Jorasses were new for me too. I had not come to revive an experience, nor did my pleasure this time lie in the exploration of new ground or the actual climbing. It was in the joy of my companion and my happiness in having one of the finest jobs in the world.... And now, back at the Eigergletscher, I wondered: Why should we not have the same luck tomorrow?

We left the Eigergletscher station at three in the morning with only one wish in our minds—for the cold which promises a fine day and keeps loose stones firmly glued in the ice. An hour later, at the foot of the face, we went through the oft-repeated actions. Out came the rope, we uncoiled it, roped up and began to climb. Our two parties, each in fine form, made brisk progress; for we knew well that on this wall speed means safety. Thus by six o'clock we had arrived at the Hinterstoisser traverse. Despite a light coating of verglas we succeeded in crossing it quickly. Leroux and myself already knew it well, since we had passed it in both directions a fortnight before, during our first, unsuccessful attempt.

But suddenly I heard voices above me. I could hardly believe my ears! Quickly I climbed on, and a hundred and twenty feet higher saw indeed two climbers, then two more. That made nine of us in all, on a face that is climbed very rarely indeed! Never had there been such a crowd, even at the time of the early attempts. Paul joined me and we stopped, dumbfounded, to watch the two ropes ahead. It was evident that they were moving very slowly, for we had caught them up quite early in the morning, whereas they had already bivouacked once on the face.

This completely spoiled our pleasure. Gone were the delights of solitude and the interest of route-finding.

Following these two ropes would be unpleasant. Gone was our speed—unless they would let us pass. More than once I have allowed parties through that were faster or in a greater hurry than my own. At any rate it was worth trying, and we climbed on to catch up the four ahead. Exactly two rope-lengths above the Hinterstoisser traverse we caught up with two very young Germans, Otto and Sepp Maag. They pointed out to us the Austrians, Buhl and Jochler.[1] Knowing Buhl by reputation I gaily hailed the leader, but was surprised to be greeted by the second. Then we told the Germans of our wish to pass them, but in vain. We could not insist, since in any case Jean Bruneau, Pierre Leroux and Guido Magnone, being a rope of three, could not go fast enough.

So we followed behind, and on the second ice slope we kept our distance. Despite their love for the hills and their enthusiasm for the Eiger face, the crampon technique of these young Germans left a lot to be desired. They had not started with Buhl and Jochler, but had been

[1] Hermann Buhl, pioneer of some astonishing climbs in the Alps, particularly in winter, reached the summit of Nanga Parbat (26,620 feet) alone on 3rd July 1953. Jochler was one of the two members of the Austro-Swiss party to reach the summit of Cho Ovu (26,756 feet) in the autumn of 1954.

extremely glad to meet them on this awe-inspiring wall;
they had tagged on behind and were following faithfully
in their steps. Their equipment was very rough and
ready; neither they nor the Austrians had really warm
clothes; their trousers were of cotton or thin cloth, their
anoraks light. While we were waiting it was almost em-
barrassing to put on our down jackets. Sepp was shod in
ski boots, and his socks, which were too short, did not join
up with the bottom of his trousers. It was certainly a fine
thing that these two brothers, aged eighteen and twenty-
three, should have the urge to climb the Eiger north face;
but their equipment came straight out of a climbing
school. Jochler in front looked rather more the part. With
a curiously shaped balaclava on his head, and his ice-axe
in his hand, he looked like a medieval man-at-arms.

At about noon we arrived at the little terrace where
Sedlmeier and Mehringer died in 1935. Midday already!
Tired of following, we stopped and ate a leisurely lun-
cheon. We had hoped, when we set off early in the
morning, to bivouac not far from the summit. When we
caught up with the Austrians and Germans that seemed
unlikely; now it was quite out of the question. It was easy
to understand the lack of speed of the two young Ger-

mans, but we could not explain the slowness of the Austrians. Hermann Buhl was very experienced and had climbed the Walker Spur under difficult conditions. He was said to be very fast; but so far it was Jochler who had done the leading.

So we waited. Precious time was slipping by, wasted. On this sinister, murderous face, the rusty pitons and rotton ropes dating from the early attempts, the stone wall which surrounded us as we ate, and which sheltered Sedlmeier and Mehringer before they died—all these combined to remind us that the moment you cease climbing towards the summit, success and safety itself are compromised. That is more than a painful and depressing impression—it is literally true. You are lost in the hollow basin of this curving wall; it is vast, and the line of advance is tortuous. Already we had passed a third of our time in horizontal traverses which did not gain us a foot of height.

We started off again. We crossed the third snow patch and arrived at the Ramp, a rocky escarpment which rises obliquely to the left. Here were the Austrians and Germans; and once again we waited, then followed leisurely. The first rope-lengths may be easy, but we knew that where the gully narrows it would be difficult, and we would have to wait again. We stopped on a narrow ledge; then, seeing that almost no progress was being made, we went on to have a look.

Buhl was struggling with the right-hand side of the narrow cleft. He drove in pitons, came back, and then started again. The real passage is on the left, but it was covered with verglas and Buhl must have wanted to avoid it. Just a little to the right it is possible to pass, as Lachenal and Terray[1] did in 1947, but Buhl was too far out to the side.

We joined the Germans at the foot of the narrow section. Just at this moment a few rays of sunshine slipping over the crest came to warm the face and melt the ice. But this was no better, for the gully was now flooded by a small waterfall from the melting of a little patch of snow one hundred and twenty feet higher. Here our friends Bruneau, Leroux and Magnone arrived, and we regained our high spirits, despite all. A rope of two can take itself seriously, but a party of five Frenchmen is incapable of striking too dramatic an attitude, however sinister the wall, however continuous the suspense or

[1] French guides, both members of the Annapurna expedition.

disquieting the promise of traditional bad weather. Bruneau's gaiety infected us all.

Jochler had by now joined Buhl, who started on an acrobatic traverse still further to the right. I was certain that it led nowhere, and that the only route lay up the waterfall. The Germans hesitated, but seeing me advance to climb the waterfall route they made up their minds; Sepp launched away at the obstacle and got up after a struggle. When it came to his turn Otto, the younger brother, turned to me without a word (he spoke no French and I no German) and passed down the end of his rope. At first I did not understand, then he signed to me to tie on. I was surprised, then disarmed by the gesture. For a moment I hesitated, then I took the rope and tied it round me. Otto went on, evidently happy that I had not refused his overture of friendship.

It was now my turn to attack. The passage was not too difficult, but I came out drenched. Paul soon joined me, followed by Buhl and Jochler, who had abandoned their attempt on the right. They did not use the rope offered by the young Germans, who seemed disappointed on this small point of pride. While I was giving a dry pullover to Sepp Maag—who was clad, to my amazement, only in a light shirt and ski anorak—Buhl and Jochler swept past without a word and hurled themselves at the next problem, once more in the lead.

A hundred and twenty feet more and we had surmounted the Ramp. We came out on a steep snow patch in the centre of an amphitheatre. It was late, and each party set about looking for a bivouac site. The Austrians and Germans, who had gone on too high, came down again; meanwhile we built ourselves a very rudimentary platform. Magnone wielded his axe lustily to flatten the ground a little, while Leroux, ingenious as ever, built a rickety stone wall. I drove in pitons to secure the party. Habran talked hard and Bruneau, when he could, got in a wise-crack which set us all laughing. Meanwhile the Germans and Austrians, sixty feet above us, maintained a cheerless silence, each in his separate corner.

Night came down over the mountains. Below, the rustic notes of the Alpine horn had ceased. Above, the lamp-lighter of the heavens had done his round. Leroux prepared a saucepan of hot drink, while the sausage, bacon, jam and dry cakes circulated. Habran quoted from his favourite author: "They enjoyed a spicy insecurity." That was how it was. Friendship kept us warm.

Then the cigarettes, smoked as we sat half reclining on our rocky couch, tasted amazingly good.

I woke up several times during the night, surprised and uneasy to find that it was not colder. The stars seemed so near that you could touch them, and the Milky Way shone with sinister brightness. Then I woke up again; the air was warm and wet when it should have been dry and cold. Later still a light veil of mist showed to the west. The stars flickered, then disappeared for good. Such a night spelt a cheerless morning, with great banks of heavy cloud borne up from behind the horizon. The sky darkened near us, ready to spill its contents upon our heads.

I shall always remember that still-born day-break! The morning before, we had launched our assault in splendid weather. Now everything was in the melting-pot. Bad weather is traditional, the guardian had said. It looks as if no one can be sure of conquering the face unless he is ready to pay the price of being caught in a bad storm.

We were now less than a thousand feet from the summit, but there were many horizontal traverses before we could win it. The wall is a trap, as we knew well. All who had been caught by storm and tried to descend had perished; safety lies towards the summit. But why talk of such things? To none of us did it ever occur to descend; each prepared to continue the climb. First the Austrians started, then the Germans followed, attached to their rope. We did not hurry, for if we went too fast we would have to wait. When we did start I cut steps up the ice slope instead of taking to the rock as they had done. The feeling of freedom, the feeling of making my own way again, was wonderful.

Soon we had caught up with the Germans. The wall was wax-coloured, and just as Jean Bruneau declared "It's going to lift" the snow began.

"I'm starting," I said to Paul, who had my rope.

"Off you go, *mon vieux*, and the best of luck!"

The climb up the side of a vertical pillar was difficult, and the frozen rock was covered with great flakes of snow driven up by the west wind. But I felt happy to be passing from inaction to action. The wait and the threat of bad weather had been agonizing. Now we at least knew where we stood, and when all was said and done the storm was not really so bad. Besides, it was in keeping with the Eiger north face. We would play the game out, and it would not be for the first time. We were in splendid form. I looked back at Jean Bruneau, last of the party and four rope-lengths behind. I was not to see him again till evening.

The limestone under its covering of snow was freezing to the touch. I made a long stride, and found the pillar bulging convex above me. I calculated my rate of progress so as to fit in with Otto, fifteen feet higher. He was climbing furiously in the attempt to go fast. Here was a piton, relic of the first ascent, and I hooked my finger into it for hold. Suddenly I heard a crack above: a block big as a milestone had given way under Otto's feet. Suspended from my finger, which remained hooked through the piton, I swung to the right to avoid the block. But it burst and split above my head, into pieces that struck me. My head swam, everything span around me... But the finger hooked through the piton still held. It was very painful, and felt as if it had been sawn through.

The world around me gradually came back into focus. I felt a sticky trickle down my face and a great weight on my shoulders. I looked at my finger, still in the piton, and felt happy and grateful that it had not given.

Then the Germans above sent down a rope; I tied myself on instinctively and climbed up. A little blood fell from my cap and reddened the snow-flecked rock. My right elbow was painful, and it was a struggle to reach the stance, where I found Otto and Sepp very upset indeed about this accident. Then I secured Paul, who climbed up to me; soon I had the joy of feeling him at my side. The snow continued.

The Germans went on, still roped to the Austrians as they had been since morning. From this point it was necessary to make a horizontal traverse of four rope-lengths to reach the last snow patch frozen into the face. It is called the Spider. I rested a moment to recover morale, then set off again. I could not see the Germans, for the visibility was limited to a few yards and the ceiling of cloud weighed heavily, lowering over our heads, seeming to stifle us. Everything was white: the rocks, Otto in front, Paul behind. The others had disappeared, blotted out against this wall that was white with snow falling thickly, ceaselessly.

In the morning I had felt almost happy that the inevitable storm had burst at last. Now, with my head aching and my elbow numb, I advanced without enthusiasm. My heart was no longer in the job; and all around was a cold, white and silent hell. The human animal in me was unhappy; the snow entered by my wrists and neck, my fingers were clumsy, my toes freezing, my damp clothes formed a creaking shell. I sensed the same reflections and the same anxieties in my companions, and in the Germans and Austrians. They, like ourselves, were no more than human.

But little by little man adapts himself, as he must. Seeing a world transformed, he gradually moulds it to become his own. Confronted by the joint forces of mountains and elements he feels born in himself a power, a balance and reserve that normally lie dormant, withdrawn, but which reveal themselves in time of need. He calmly faces the problems. And so it was here. A moment before, our movements had nothing spontaneous about them, the animal in us groaned and struggled. Despite the cold, despite the whirling snow and the biting wind, we found life returning gradually as we reached a harder passage—the exit from our shelf on to the Spider. Little by little we were warmed; an irresistible strength flowed in us, a strength which we must distribute through our body to combat the wind, the snow and

the cold. This was no passing exaltation; it was the discovery by man that this wind, this snow and this cold are
obstacles, but not enemies. Thanks to this power within
him he can succeed in the most daring undertakings,
provided he is prudent. It was in vain that the avalanches
swept ceaselessly down; we had noted with care that the
funnel down which they poured was interrupted by a
jutting ledge. We made use of this and crept in under it.
For a moment we disappeared under the flow of snow
sweeping smoothly over us; the rope tightened between
one man and the next as he struggled, half choked, and
clasped the rock with his fingers. His life depended on
that grasp. Then he emerged on the other side, and the
great powdery mass continued to flow down.

To lessen the danger Otto gave me his rope and asked
me to secure him. Just at that moment the elements were
particularly savage; avalanches were falling at an unbe-
lievable rate. When he had reached a rather less exposed
spot he secured me in turn. In this fashion we traversed
towards the middle of the ice slope of the Spider, which
was less swept than the flanks, since it was slightly convex.
But what a void yawned a hundred and fifty feet below!
Slowly the tiny human forms moved upward, while from

time to time an avalanche came spouting down from the couloirs above. Then the whole line of us at long intervals crouched against the glassy surface; each fought silently with all his strength to avoid being dragged off.

It took hours to make six rope-lengths of height. Three hundred feet above me was Buhl, three hundred below was Bruneau. It was a fearful battle, a struggle both personal and collective. Each one of us, and so the whole rope, advanced almost imperceptibly.

Above the Spider the normal route was swept by avalanches, and the Austrians had to pass a hundred and twenty feet to the right. But by the time I had climbed two rope-lengths up and arrived at the top of the ice slope, reached by Buhl an hour before, the avalanches had become less frequent and then finally stopped. All was now quiet again. Tired of waiting I unroped from the Germans, who were still roped to the Austrians, and started up to the left on the route taken by the first party to climb the face. I cut some steps and felt an enormous pleasure in doing so. At the end of the pitch I drove in a piton and was astonished that it sang as it went in; this very rarely happens in limestone, and meant that it was fixed firmly. Habran came up to me. So far the couloir had remained quiet, and I reached and crossed it. It gleamed like a bobsleigh run set almost vertically upright. I climbed on a few more yards. The rock step above me was steep and iced, but not impossible, and I knew that two pitons left by the first party should make the exit from it easier. Above that the angle eased off.

But just as I started up I heard a whistle like an express train. I leaped six feet to the left of the couloir's centre and was smothered in the fine snow of an avalanche from above. For a moment everything was quiet, then another avalanche enveloped me in its cloud. Then a third fall, less powdery, more moisture-laden, slid heavily down. An enormous mass of snow shook me and slipped smoothly down my back, piling up on my head, freezing my lungs and flowing on as if it would never stop. It was only by flattening myself against the vertical rock and clinging to it that I could avoid being torn away.

Magnone joined me between two avalanches, while Paul remained at the firm piton to secure us. But by now the falls were coming down faster and faster. Never, even on Annapurna, had I seen anything like it. First a mighty puff of wind, which shook us where we stood; then we were caught in the waves of snow dust, finally to be enveloped in the tons of accumulated white snow. We were mere straws, held in place by fingers that clutched at rounded, frozen holds.

Guido and myself could, if we wished, go down between two avalanches and rejoin Habran, Leroux, and Bruneau, then follow the right-hand route; but this would take too long, and it was already late. In an hour darkness would have fallen. We therefore called to the Germans and Austrians; they were invisible behind a convex projection, but we knew that they were some sixty feet above us and on our right. Because of the noise of avalanches and wind we could scarcely hear each other, even shouting our hardest. However, finally they understood and let down a rope. But then I had to go and get it on the other side of the couloir; and having got it I had to pull myself up. I had thought that the Germans and Austrians would be able to give me some help, but this proved impossible because of the noise and the fact that we could not see each other. As for the rope, it was caked in ice as an electric wire is surrounded with insulating rubber. Indeed it was no rope at all, but a stiff, iced hawser. It was impossible even to have a twist round my wrists. Would I ever succeed in climbing sixty feet simply on the strength of my hands, without the least respite, up this smooth wall? Yet it was the only way of avoiding the couloir, down which the avalanches poured ceaselessly.

For a long moment I hesitated. The avalanches continued. Then, quite calmly, I made my decision. I was afraid, but there was no alternative.

So up I went. Immediately after the latest snow-slide I grasped the ice rope (for it was no longer hemp), traversed across the couloir and began to climb very fast. I would not let go, I knew that, but I must climb fast, for one cannot hold long in this position. My whole existence centred on a rather desperate and yet very clear-headed effort to lock my fingers round this iced and terribly slippery thread. My whole body was suspended from my fingers, and my fingers were growing tired. Will-power exhausts itself when the muscles refuse to obey, as I knew very well. But I knew also that to climb sixty feet up a dry rope of half an inch in diameter is not too easy, even in good weather. In this case it was no rope at all but a glass thread, and we had already been climbing for two days without stopping. Below me in the couloir the avalanches continued to fall.

Somehow I reached the stance where Jochler and

Sepp Maag were holding the rope. I thanked them, and answered their smile. They patted me in friendly fashion on the back. Then Otto, who was a few feet below, joined us while Jochler climbed up towards Buhl. We then quickly brought up Magnone, Habran, Leroux and Bruneau. We kept them on a very tight rope, indeed we almost pulled them, for I knew what the conditions were like. Our nylon rope had remained supple, and this eased our manœuvres in various ways. One by one they arrived, very thankful to be out of that miserable abyss! And by the time the whole party was reassembled, the happiness of being together again cheered us once more. The snow continued while we set about preparing our bivouac.

The Austrians settled down a rope-length above us. The Germans, almost at the end of their tether, preferred to remain with us in the relative comfort of our soaked down jackets. They had no bivouac equipment, no clothing apart from their thin shirts and their cotton anoraks, a short waistcoat and the sweater which I had given to Sepp on the previous day. And since last evening they had eaten nothing. We ourselves were soaked; for the snow had long ago melted at the warmth of our skin and trickled down our backs and along our arms. We had set out with the idea of bivouacking once only; and our provisions, luckily planned on an ample scale, were beginning to run short.

All seven of us sat there, with our legs dangling or in stirrups of frozen rope, on these two miserable ledges, two staircase steps worn and rounded and sloping outward, yet somehow suspended on this gigantic wall. The higher one was comparatively spacious, about eight inches wide and three feet long. We managed to squeeze five on to it: Jean Bruneau was on the extreme right, the two Germans between him and me, while Pierre Leroux succeeded in sitting on my left. On the tiny step below, Paul Habran and Guido Magnone snuggled against each other, with their backs to our legs. We were all attached to pitons, like goats to a stake, in case we slipped or anyone went to sleep. And we were covered with a small piece of "vinzle" cloth which Guido had had the brilliant idea of bringing. This was held in place by pitons and stretched over our heads, making a sort of roof.

Meanwhile the avalanches continued to slither down the couloir. Here they were light and infrequent. They slid hissing over our cloth roof, though a part succeeded in piling up between our backs and the rock wall. From time to time the west wind brought up a sprinkling of powder snow which got in everywhere, down our necks (despite our hoods), into pockets and sleeves and gloves, between our clothes and into our boots. Our bivouac looked like a village laid waste by storm.

And yet, despite our anxiety and the close quarters, a spark of gaiety warmed us. We had strength in numbers and still felt fit. Paul and Guido made an inventory of our provisions. Pierrot, balancing like a trapeze artist, managed to put a saucepan of snow on the stove, which I was balancing awkwardly on my knees. The match-box was wet, but after a number of failures a tiny flame hesitated, flickered, made an island in the prevailing dampness, and like a little queen shed its gleam of joy upon the world. Otto and Sepp expressed their happiness at being with us, while Jean announced in his even, cheerful voice that "this sets a new tradition." We shared out some sweets, some pieces of sugar, crumbled biscuits and a little tepid water from the melted snow.

At about 2 A.M. there was a sudden change of weather. The snow stopped and it became freezing cold. The din overhead ceased, the west wind gave way to a wind from the north which beat back the clouds and piled them in the valley, reinstated the stars in the sky but brought a bitter chill to earth below. To-morrow it would be fine, but at the moment each blast was like a hatchet blow. With the crack of a whip it would come beating against the wall, shaking our ice-gripped encampment. We shivered violently, our wet clothes stiffened, our feet froze, everything became hard and brittle. The cold bit into our sleepy bodies; we crouched and cowered. The avalanches, which still came down at intervals, were pulverized immediately by the wind. This raised our hopes, but wore down our resistance. The rock wall gleamed white and luminous through the darkness. Above all we must not go to sleep! For if you go to sleep you give up the struggle, and if you give up the struggle you risk going to sleep for ever. How long the eagerly awaited day took to dawn! These were the hardest hours, for we must watch and wait as I had watched in the crevasse below the summit of Annapurna.... The night was endless.

And yet, now that sleep and death were resisted, the blessed moment came at last when the white, silent landscape was filled with light. It was the third day. The

Eiger, a pyramid of black rock, was now a peak of spotless snow! The sun remained hidden behind the Mitteleggi ridge, but it reassured us with its presence. The cold was very keen, certainly below −10°C. The face was grey, but not without its own beauty. Our wretched night of inaction was over, and we were about to climb again. To-morrow we would be having rolls and coffee for breakfast.

Even more on this day than the others, I would have liked to make my own way through this white world. Strange and difficult as it was, I yet felt a love for it, since it was the world of high summits and elemental forces. But sixty feet above us the Austrians were preparing to climb the vertical rise which dominated our position. Foreseeing that the struggle would be severe they asked us for pitons and took in the rope to secure Sepp, as he climbed up to them, taking all that we had. Then Buhl started. He found himself immediately on very difficult ground, for underneath the snow the rock was covered with a shining layer of hard, thick ice carpeting the whole surface. The feet skated off, the hands slid from the holds, every crack was blocked up, every hold levelled out. It was very difficult to drive pitons in; the hammer tapped, dug in, tired, tapped askew, and flaked off a chunk of thick ice. The whole body would slide, suspended from its piton. Then it would recover and hoist itself up; for a moment the laboured breathing would stop altogether. Then the hammer would dig out a hold, push off a layer of snow covering a slab, clean out another hold, and the foot would succeed in driving a crampon point into the verglas while numb fingers freed a crack of its ice and drove in another piton. Buhl gained a foot, then a yard; his feet slipped again and he was off altogether, but the pitons held. The cold was terrible, the sky very clear. Our feet were frozen and our muscles stiff, the whole human machine was petrified; our clothes were like a suit of armour, our rope a steel thread. But heart and will held on, invincible. Buhl advanced slowly, and with wonderful doggedness succeeded in climbing the rise. Jochler joined him and continued in the lead. The Germans followed, then my turn came to start. We all used the ropes to go faster. A rocky spur jutting from the wall like a ship's prow provided a good resting-place for a moment or two; the view downwards from it was staggering. Pierrot and Jean were still at the bivouac site, a tiny nest lost upon this enormous panel of snow. How had we been able to seat seven for a whole night on that wretched ledge where even the two of them seemed so awkwardly placed? The glimpse downwards filled us with confidence for the future: we had come up from there, and nothing more above could stop us.

By a pendulum movement on the rope we landed in a couloir, but this was in the sun, and the snow was melting in its warmth. The avalanches started again, this time not powdery but wet and heavy, carrying stones with them. On the traverse Guido lost a crampon; and in the couloir an axe slipped from the hands of one of the Germans. At each rope-length the climbers were secured by a piton driven in.

We made slow progress, but little by little the angle eased and we could go faster. We still had to be extremely careful in the dangerous couloir. Guido was hit on the lip by a falling stone. He was expertly held by Paul. At last we were on the final slope, covered in the lower part by wind-crusted snow, but in hard ice higher up. I found pleasure in the effort of chipping steps for Guido's left foot that had lost its crampon. This held us up a bit, but it mattered little. By the time I surmounted the cornice of the Mitteleggi ridge the Germans and Austrians had already reached the summit and were descending on the other side. That was the last I was to see of them.

My companions joined me and we went on. The climb up the last three hundred feet of ridge was sheer joy. At about 6:00 P.M. we were on top of the Eiger. The air was cold, but this summit air tasted good. As far as the eye could reach a sea of cloud stretched in white billows; the higher summits, resplendent in their robes of fresh snow, alone emerged, like lands surviving above a flood which had drowned the earth.

Here Paul gave us a surprise. At the bivouac the evening before he had cheated a little in the distribution of food; he had kept some back. Now he emptied his sack and handed round the last rations: a few more sweets, some lumps of sugar and broken biscuits.

"I kept this in case we had to bivouac again," he said, with a happy grin.

But at last the struggle was over, and we looked at each other with some emotion. During these three days nobody had given in, and good humour had reigned throughout. We had remained a happy party. Why should we be so happy after so hard a climb? For three days we had met nothing but difficulties, cold and storm, everything that men shrink from. It was not only the airy overhangs or the acrobatic corners, for how could these alone have produced this feeling of joy? I did not think they could be the reason, and now it seemed to me that the Eiger climbed in good weather would have been a lesser achievement. In this case we had committed no folly, no imprudence. We had made every preparation to succeed, and we had succeeded. Throughout this ascent, this snow and this storm, we had come to recognize from the bottom of our inmost hearts a great sense of fulfillment: of a life linked closely with the elements, a sense of comradeship, a taste for things which, when you have once tasted them, can never be replaced.

For a moment more we stood and contemplated the world apart which is the world of high mountains. All fatigue had vanished. Below us the sea of cloud was arched by the caress of the west wind, like a cat that is stroked.

But it was late, and we must think about leaving the

summit. We had only two hours of daylight in which to reach the Eigergletscher station. We descended the ordinary route at a run, with life singing through our veins as it had done that morning, the day before, and the day before that.

Life, the luxury of being!

The Brotherhood of the Rope: Techniques and Tools

I. LEARNING TO CLIMB

Climbing Is a Natural Instinct

I HAD, first of all, to learn how to climb.

I knew how to climb as a child. Instinctively, without having learned, all children climb walls, windows and trees. They do so for the pleasure of climbing and for the joy of discovery, of seeing further. Is this not exactly the same reward that climbers seek in high mountains?

It happens very often, however, that between our fifth and our twentieth birthdays, education, society and easy living weaken and little by little kill the instinctive desires and spontaneous impulses of our childhood. Farewell climbing, escape and discovery!

And if by chance one day, kindled by some wondrous and unexpected spark, these desires and impulses of childhood reappear, the instinct is dead and we must learn to climb all over again. This happened to me, as it does to many boys.

Thus it is that the climbing instincts of our childhood develop. The windows, trees and walls which we cheerfully climbed at the age of five or ten have now become the Matterhorn, Mont Blanc or the Himalayas. Our puny, childish muscles have grown stronger, and so has our will. In like measure has the need in us for fresh air, discovery and conquest crystallized. Austerity has become our way of life, and to make room for it, we have put aside sensitiveness and softness, resolved to remain strong on the threshold of life.

In quenching this thirst for discovery, in guiding this fervor which inspires the early part of a man's life, the mountains have provided for me what others have found in the sea, the air, the desert or the polar regions. These "wide open spaces," which allow a man to find the truth in himself and to develop it in all its fullness, are as close to each other in spirit as they are different to outside view. The externals matter little; are not mountaineers, sailors, airmen and explorers closely akin, for all the variety of their clothes? Are not they all carried forward by the same impulse?

Friend, Come Climbing with Me

You love mountains, or rather you have a longing for them. Many times you have caught a glimpse of their beauty, from the bottom of a valley....

But today, that is no longer sufficient. You are twenty; that is to say, your body is almost completely formed, you have a good set of muscles (but not much endurance yet, so you will have to go easily at first). Perhaps you are still studying, or you have a job which keeps you in the city when sometimes you would like to leave it, especially when spring comes, with its fine, warm weather which brings out the need for the simplicity of nature and for truth.

Perhaps then, persuaded by friends, you have already tried your hand at climbing; you have touched red granite or white limestone, dead rock apparently, and suddenly you felt under your fingertips a strength quite new to you, a strength clamoring to be released. One day, probably on a weekend, you left the noisy streets behind to follow a little path which led you to the foot of a cliff or rock pinnacle.

Clumsily you uncoiled a rope. Feeling happy, rather scared, rather moved, you roped yourself up, or probably you were roped up. Your friend took the lead. Fearfully you watched him climb, then an angle of rock hid him and at that moment, you realized better what a rope means. First of all you clutched it more firmly, and when you raised your eyes to watch it rise up the rock face, this nylon thread acquired tremendous value for you and you understood the full beauty of this link.

Then the rope grew taut and you began to climb, and you were at times glad to see this spiritual link before you in concrete form.

At night you went home, having discovered a real happiness, bearing on man's fundamental nature. The next day and the following days were spent thinking of that first weekend. Now the memories of the peaks you glimpsed from the bottom of the valley and those of your first climb are interwoven and you begin to plan....

With the help of competent friends, you are going to acquire some equipment, fine equipment which you are already contemplating with a loving eye: the ice-axe—your ice-axe; the rope—your rope; your crampons, your rucksack; and you eagerly look forward to your departure for the mountains.

II. CLIMBING EQUIPMENT

On its quality depend:

1) your safety,
2) your pleasure.

THE ROPE

Formerly, manila ropes were used for snow climbs and hemp ropes over rock. Today, both manila and hemp are overshadowed by nylon, which offers considerable advantages: toughness, lightness and flexibility when the rope is wet. Manila and hemp ropes had necessarily to have three strands. Nylon ropes can be woven, since nylon does not decay. Nevertheless, three-stranded ropes are preferable, even when made of nylon, because, in contrast to woven ropes, which are smooth, they have a rough surface and thus offer a better grip to the hands.

Climbing Rope: This is the rope normally used for "roping up." If made of nylon, the diameter should be ⅜ inch to ⁷⁄₁₆ inch. The length varies with the length of the climb and the numbers involved—65, 100 or 130 feet, sometimes 200 feet for long climbs.

Rappel Rope: From ¼ to ⁵⁄₁₆ inch in diameter, if of nylon, and 130 to 200 feet long, these ropes are normally used for *rappel*[1] descents. Thanks to nylon, they can also be used as climbing ropes provided they are doubled. On very long trips, as on the North Face of the Grandes Jorasses, I have always used a *rappel* rope doubled. In this way *rappel* ropes can also be used for artificially aided climbing. I have used a cord 100 feet long for pulling up rucksacks on very acrobatic pitches.

Rope Rings: These are made of cord ⅛ to ³⁄₁₆ inches in diameter, and are passed round a rocky projection or piton to support the *rappel* rope. These rings are aban-

---

[1] For the convenience of readers there is a glossary of technical mountaineering terms at the end of this book.

doned in place after use. Rope rings should be fastened with a square knot, which should be carefully checked.

Rope Maintenance: The maintenance of mountain ropes consists chiefly in drying them out at once, on returning from a climb, if they are wet.

During the climb, they must not be trodden on or dragged over rocks or snow. With nylon ropes, *rappel* descents must not be too rapid if karabiners are used. The heat generated by the friction of the rope on the karabiner tends to melt and weaken the nylon.

Coiling the Ropes: Coiling a rope must be done in a practical way, i.e., the climber must be able to coil and uncoil ropes very quickly where the space is very restricted.

THE ICE-AXE

This is the tool but at the same time the friend of the climber. The first use to which it can be put is that of a walking stick on mountain paths and, above all, on snow and ice slopes. The ice-axe can also be used to cut steps in ice, to ensure the safety of the party, to stop falls and to act as a brake on descents.

The ice-axe should not be as short as the fashion has

recently been, or as long as alpenstocks were in the early days of Alpine climbing. The usual length varies between 29½ and 37½ inches. The ice-axe, standing upright against the climber's leg, should just reach his hand when the arm is hanging down normally.

(On certain specialized climbs, where rock predominates, an ice-axe which can be taken to pieces may be used.)

The climber must get into the habit of gripping the ice-axe firmly in the hand, so as to be able to dispense with a sling, which is always a source of accidents.

CRAMPONS

These may be twelve-pointed, but crampons with ten points are quite adequate, even on the steepest ice. The main thing is to use them well, and for that, one's ankles must be both very supple and very strong. For certain climbs of a mainly rocky nature, light crampons are adequate.

PITONS

The use of pitons entered mountain climbing technique in a similar way to the use of crampons.

Pitons are metal blades of various sizes, intended to be driven into cracks in the rock or into ice, as much for security as for aiding further progress. There are two kinds of pitons, rock pitons and ice pitons.

Rock pitons, forged in one piece—the ring is cut out of the blade—are of soft iron, so that they can mold themselves to the unevennesses of the cracks without losing too much of their rigidity. They are made with such precision that they can be used one on top of the other, doubling up in a broad crack. By using special steel, pitons can be made very strong and yet fairly light. Their average weight varies between 2½ and 3½ ounces. Pitons must be suited to the climb as planned: horizontal, vertical, extra flat, extra short, U-shaped, ringed, etc.

Ice pitons are generally in two parts, the blade and the ring. They are made of special steel, harder than that used for rock pitons, but not tempered, so as not to be brittle. The very fine point alone is slightly tempered. The blade is about 10 inches long, .8 inch wide and .2 inch thick. It is flat so that it will press perpendicularly against the ice in the direction of the slope and consequently in the direction of the strain. The piton is fine-pointed and sharp-edged, so as to penetrate the ice swiftly, without flaking it away. In order to prevent its being pulled out of its seat, an ice piton is barbed. Finally, it is rigid, so as to penetrate the ice perpendicularly without bending. The ring is of steel wire with a diameter of about 1.6 inches.

On ice, certain U-shaped pitons, 10 inches long, may also be used.

On certain exceptionally difficult climbs, other types of piton have been used, especially pitons with extensions.

THE HAMMER

This must be fairly heavy, stout and stocky, so as to have plenty of power behind it.

KARABINERS

These snap-rings are generally made of steel, but are sometimes of duralumin, which has the advantage of lightness. But as the latter are less safe, they should be used rather for rope maneuvers than for security.

STIRRUPS

To be really useful, these should be two-storied. The duralumin footrests should neither be too broad, which causes jamming, nor too narrow for the foot to enter easily.

III. PERSONAL EQUIPMENT

Personal equipment should be warm, light, strong and of first-class quality.

Changes of temperature occur very suddenly in the mountains. The climber must be able to take off or put on clothes very rapidly. His equipment will be severely tested, and it must be in perfect condition before every climb. There must be no holes in the gloves, no open seams in the boots, no vibram soles coming away; pullovers and jackets must not be too short. Climbing clothes in poor shape may lead to accidents.

CLOTHING AND FOOTWEAR

The socks must be long. No bare skin should appear between socks and trousers when a leg is raised. Short socks should not be worn.

The "stop-tout": Ankle gaiters were formerly used, but the "stop-tout" is preferable. It keeps out snow and small stones on the approach. It is a poplin gaiter, with elastic top and bottom, and is completely watertight.[1]

Trousers: These are shaped like knickers and are joined to the leg four inches below the knee. Trousers which are baggy at the ankle should be avoided. They get wet easily in snow and catch in crampons.

Trousers may be of velvet material for pure rock climbing (e.g., in the Dolomites), but they should always be of warm, strong cloth for climbing at high altitudes and particularly on snow. For certain lengthy climbs, long trousers are recommended.

Sweater: The sweater must extend well down the body so as to protect the stomach and the small of the back. A down jacket is not always necessary, but in view of its very light weight and its small volume when folded, it is very pleasant to have one, for it insures a gratifying warmth.

Smock or Anorak: This must be of closely woven cloth or thick, waterproof poplin. It must extend well down the body—nearly halfway down the thighs and not

---

[1] *Translator's note:* This type of gaiter has lately become fashionable at Chamonix and Courmayeur.

merely to the waist like the blouse of earlier days. When climbing, a man raises his arms frequently; this in turn pulls up his clothes. If the shirt, pull-over or sweater is too short, his stomach and back will be exposed to the air. The trousers will tend to slip in the opposite direction; for this reason, suspenders are recommended.

Gloves and mittens: It is pleasant to wear a pair of coarse woolen gloves, long enough to cover the wrists, and a pair of mittens over them.

Headgear: Everyone has his own favorite—hat, beret, balaclava, cap, ear-protector. The important point is to protect the ears; it is also pleasant to have a peak to one's headgear in rain or snow.

Shirts: These must be very warm and fitted with pockets. They must extend very low.

Snow glasses: As with headgear, each climber has his own preference; the important point is that the eyes must be completely protected.

Boots: Formerly climbing boots were studded with metal tricounis and clinker nails. This kind of sole has now been superseded by vibram soles. Two pairs of boots are advised:

For rock climbing, a relatively snug-fitting pair, light, laced very low, and with soles with little overlap;

For snow, slightly larger boots, so that the climber can wear two pairs of socks without discomfort, especially when crampons have to be worn. The latter have straps which inevitably tend to hinder blood circulation and so lead to frostbite.

RUCKSACKS

Rucksacks with rigid frames are being used less and less; for climbing, they are a mistake, as they are stiff, cumbersome, and above all, very badly designed. (Generally speaking, they were designed by manufacturers who never wore them.) The shape of these rucksacks is influenced by custom which, as always in such cases, it is difficult to destroy.

The mountain rucksack must never resemble a pear in shape, hanging down the back as far as the buttocks, and thus compelling the climber to lean forward in an unnatural posture. It must be longer than it is broad and wider at the top than at the bottom, thus corresponding to human anatomy, in which the width across the shoulders is greater than at the waist.

During the last few years, rucksacks with flexible frames have been made. These are lighter and much more convenient than the heavy and cumbersome sacks with stiff frames. According to the climb he has planned, the mountaineer should use either a flexible-frame rucksack or a rucksack with no frame. The best are the Super-Vallée (flexible frame) and the Super-Altitude (no frame), made by Lafuma.

The following items must always find a place in the rucksack:

1. A spare pair of gloves

2. An extra pair of socks

3. A spare pair of goggles, well protected in a metal case

4. Field dressing

5. Safety pins

6. Water-tight matchbox

7. Three or four pitons

8. Two or three karabiners

9. A little light rope

You may also take:

1. A map of the range
2. A compass (but you must know how to use it before you need it—before being lost in a fog, for example).
3. A camera. The mountains are so beautiful, and it is so satisfying to have pleasant souvenirs of your climbs.

BIVOUAC EQUIPMENT

This includes the following items:

Long, rubberized nylon smocks. There are some very light ones, weighing only a few ounces, which occupy a negligible amount of space when properly folded. They can also be used as protective clothing outside bivouacs in rain or snow, since they extend well below the knees.

"Elephant's feet." These are rubberized nylon bags, of the same material as the smocks, which can be joined to them by snap-studs when bivouacking.

Down jacket. This should be a long jacket and not a blouse which stops at the waist.

A Zdarsky sack-tent may also be used when bivouacking.

RULES FOR EQUIPMENT

Do not encumber yourself unnecessarily. Weight is the great enemy. On the other hand, do not leave anything out. Equipment must be suited to the projected climb, whether it is a pure rock climb, ice climb, mixed climb, medium-altitude or high-altitude climb, a climb with an easy return home, or with a tricky one, a one-day climb or one lasting several days and involving bivouacking.

IV. THE TECHNIQUE OF MOUNTAIN CLIMBING

The Joy of Climbing Well

Technique is not an end in itself. There is, all the same, a great satisfaction in making a gesture or a movement, or in carrying out an exercise, *well.* Technique is one of the means of communicating with mountains, not with their beauty or their grandeur, but with their raw material—snow, ice or rock—in the way that an artisan communicates with the wood or iron on which he is working.

The climber is face to face with the rock up which he

wants to climb. To do this, he must make certain gestures, just as a sculptor must, when working on his block of stone. There is contact between the flesh of the man, controlled by his mind, and matter. That is the important point. Touching fine granite is pleasant and reassuring like touching a piece of fine wood. Perhaps there is even a sensual side to it.

To do anything *well* is important. Once again, technique is not the object of climbing, but pleasure in technique is an extra satisfaction to be added to all the pleasures our beloved mountains give us. In every domain, work well done is fine work, work done without cheating, in which what is approximately right will not do.

Of course, technique is a poor thing, even a wretched thing, when separated from the heart which has guided it; this is true in rock climbing, or playing a piano, or building a cathedral. But at the bottom of a man's being, there is always a sensitive element which has demanded a fervent and passionate apprenticeship before it becomes efficient and develops into a form of beauty. Among mountaineers, too, there is such a thing as style and it can be said, without overestimating its importance, that the presence of style is a sign of quality. When I was myself learning to climb, I had occasion to watch some of the great guides at work on ice as well as on rock. It was fine to see, and they must have felt, within themselves, a gentle glow of satisfaction, an un-expressed approval as their gestures unfolded and as their movements followed smoothly on. They seemed to flow as spring water flows from a rock, running gently along the hollows and skirting the obstacles, choosing the best course offered by the lay of the land.

Roping Up

Roping up is a safety measure which must never be ne-glected.

The normal rope consists of three people, but a rope of two, although less safe, permits swifter progress.

KNOTS

The rope around the body must be firm and tight, so that the loop cannot slip. Knots must always be checked, for bad roping can lead to accidents.

Knots to be used are:

The overhand knot,

The double overhand knot, which allows a loop to be
passed over the shoulder,

The bowline, which, although very firm, can be easily
untied, even if the rope has been pulled taut,

The "baldric,"[1] which is used more and more, as it sim-
plifies rope work.

Rock Technique

1. BASIC RULES

Consider—look ahead. Before attempting a pitch, go over
it first in your head; that is to say, work out the movements in succession and the effort required till the next
stage. Hands and feet should then merely carry out
movements which have already been thought out.

Before attacking a crack or a chimney, the climber
looks at it, takes its measure, not with any feeling of hos-
tility, but frankly and openly, as equal to equal.

---

[1] *Translator's note:* This is a loop around the waist, joined by a loop or
loops over the shoulder.

Climb calmly. Each movement should be deliberate and confident, and should rhythmically follow the preceding one.

Save your strength. Climb as much as possible with your legs. Co-ordinate your muscular efforts to try to achieve rhythm in your climbing by making your movements automatic.

Remain constantly on the alert.

2. USE OF HOLDS

The strain put onto a hold must always be perpendicular to it.

Before using a hold, make sure it is firm. Do not forget that earth, grass, ice or water in a hold diminish its value considerably.

3. FREE CLIMBING

A. OPEN FACE CLIMBING

This includes all climbing on the outside faces of rocks. The main types of difficulty encountered are: walls, slabs, *arêtes* and shelves.

The normal means of overcoming these rock formations are vertical climbing, adherence and opposition.

1. Vertical climbing

Climb as you would a ladder, well balanced on your legs, without hanging on your arms. Above all, climb smoothly, making your movements follow on each other so that they are not rough or jerky.

Keep your body well away from the rock face. Beginners tend to cling to the rock and to try to reach holds at arm's length. In this position, they lack elbow room, cannot see the holds, and cannot use their legs for climbing. Also, they have no lateral balance and are soon paralyzed.

Avoid seeking hand holds too high; keep your hands as low as possible. Hands should be used only to maintain fore-and-aft and lateral balance.

Bring your legs up as high as possible, letting them bear as much of the weight of your body as you can. This is entirely normal, as legs are much stronger than arms.

Keep your weight on three points of contact.

Keep your arms and legs slightly apart to obtain greater stability.

Use your knees as little as possible.

Avoid as much as possible pulling yourself jerkily upwards by your hands, as this exhausts your arms very quickly.

2. *Adherence*

This depends on the nature of the rock. The more fine-grained the rock is, the better the adherence obtained. A fairly safe means of obtaining foot adherence is afforded nowadays by using vibram soles.

3. *Opposition*

This is forced adherence by pushing and pulling different parts of the body in opposite directions simultaneously, as, for example, when pulling backwards with the hands and pushing forwards with the feet against the rock.

B. CRACK AND CHIMNEY CLIMBING

This includes climbing rocky formations like chimneys, cracks, and open corners, in which progress is made "within" the rock; that is, inside these clefts. The technique is difficult and does not come entirely naturally. Those who are badly versed in it waste much effort in their climbing. It is even more essential in this form of climbing than in open face climbing to co-ordinate and synchronize your movements properly.

1. *Chimneys*

These are deep cracks into which the climber must penetrate if he is to advance. He makes use of the "chimneying" technique. He acts as if he were trying to push apart the two walls of the crack which comprises the chimney. According to the width of the chimney, he pushes in opposite directions as follows:

Broad chimney............back and feet
Medium chimney.........feet and hands
Narrow chimney..........back and knees
Very narrow chimney .....knees and feet

In very broad chimneys, this chimneying is transversal, in that the right hand and right foot push against the left hand and left foot.

2. *Cracks*

These are very narrow chimneys into which the body cannot enter. They are climbed by various forms of jamming with feet and hands.

Jamming: A foot or a fist is placed where the crack narrows, and the moment pressure is put on the foot or weight on the fist, jamming automatically takes place. Arms, fists, fingers, legs or feet can also be used for artificial jamming. The principle is the same as for chimneying. The arms, between the hand and the elbow, can be used, for example as a lever in a broad crack, and the ends of the fingers and the back of the hand in a narrow one, pressure being exerted at both ends as if to force apart the two sides of the crack.

Lay-back Ascent: This method of moving up a crack is performed by a combined opposition of feet and hands. The climber pushes strongly with his feet and at the same time pulls himself up with his hands, as if he were trying to pull away the rock face.

4. Artificial Aids to Rock Climbing

A. STANDING ON SHOULDERS

The first man on the rope stands on the shoulders of the second man, who is firmly settled against a projecting rock or a piton.

Do not hesitate to use this method very freely, for it eases the first man's work by allowing him to save his strength and gain time.

B. PITON TECHNIQUE

This technique, first used in the Limestone Alps, where walls are vertical and sometimes overhanging, has been greatly developed in recent years and has made it possible to master the last great problem climbs in the Alps. This difficult technique demands much practice. When it is well used, it is very safe, but slow. It should be resorted to only when all means of free climbing have been exhausted.

Placing the pitons: Select one suitable for the crack, and put it in as high as possible, so as to use the minimum number.

The climber can tell by the sound the piton gives out as it is driven in, whether it is firmly fixed or not. A clear, sharp note reveals that the piton has been firmly driven in. A hollow, dull sound betrays a bad piton, which should not be trusted. Pitons should normally be inserted point downwards, but some pitons, planted upside down in overhangs as steep as ceilings, succeed in catching very firmly in cracks and holding fast.

The use of pitons. Pitons are used in the following ways:

1. *Direct pull.* The leading climber pulls himself up by means of the piton he has just planted, the second man on the rope holds the leader up to the level of the piton by keeping the rope taut.

2. *Traversing.* The use of pitons allows climbers to carry out oblique and even horizontal traverses across walls which cannot be attempted by ordinary climbing methods. This method is chiefly used for pendulum traverses, on completely smooth walls. The *rappel* rope is threaded through a piton placed as high as possible over the pitch to be crossed. The higher the piton, the easier the traverse.

   It is also possible for the climber to grasp the climbing rope and swing himself across, keeping a grip on both ends of the rope.

3. *Climbing with two ropes:* This method, used on exceptionally difficult pitches, allows the leader to climb completely smooth faces which are vertical or even overhanging, and devoid of any holds, but offering a

crack. The climber, roped up on two ropes, of different color or diameter to prevent confusion, passes them alternately over a number of pitons which he inserts above him. If the wall to be ascended in this way is quite smooth or overhanging, it is helpful to place stirrups on the karabiners.

C. THROWING THE ROPE

To climb a pitch which is completely smooth and offers no cracks, the only remaining device is throwing the rope.

Short-Distance Throw: The rope, doubled, must be thrown so as to encircle a projecting rock. The climber then pulls himself up with his arms. This method is used, for example, on the summit block of the Aiguille de Roc.

Long-Distance Throw: Here it is no longer a question of lassoing a rocky projection, but of throwing a rope over an *arête*. A cord, weighted with a karabiner, or better still a lead weight, is flung across, attached to a rappel rope by means of a reef knot. The rappel rope is attached to a climbing rope. The rope must be made firm on the other side of the *arête* and the climber must then pull himself up. This maneuver must be carried out decidedly and quickly so as to remain as short a time as possible in this exhausting and unsafe position. This procedure is used, for instance, on the Aiguille de la République.

D. "TYROLIENNES"

This method is used to cross from one needle to another by means of the rope. The rope can be thrown across directly or preceded by a weighted cord. Once the rope has been caught, it is fastened and made firm. There are two ways of crossing:

1. In the sitting position, used for short distances. The climber sits on the rope and crosses over with his body leaning slightly forwards.

2. In the hanging position. A knee is passed over the rope and the climber pulls himself across with his hands.

5. DESCENT

A. NORMAL METHODS

1. *Descent on easy terrain:* Face the valley. The weight is carried on the palms of the hands. Do not sit down.

2. *Descent over fairly difficult rock:* Descend sideways, hands very low, body well away from the rock.

3. *Descent over difficult rock:* Face the rock. Keep the hands very low, legs apart, body well clear of the rock.

B. RAPPEL DESCENT

Double the rope and hang it over a projecting rock. (If there is none, use a piton.) Descend by holding onto both halves of the rope. Once you have gotten down, pull on one end; the other end goes up, passes around the rock or piton, and falls at the climber's feet.

1. Choosing a Site for a Rappel

(a) *On a projecting rock:* choose a firm rock, the sides of which are not too sharp (or they will cut the rope) or too smooth (or they will let the rope slip over). Pass a rope ring around the rock (make sure it cannot slip off). The ring should be broad enough to be stable. Never use old, abandoned rope for rings, which cannot insure complete safety.

(b) *On a piton:* if there is no suitable rock, drive in a firm piton. Avoid threading the rope through the hole in the piton, unless you have ringed pitons. Pass a rope ring through the piton hole. If need be, use a karabiner.

2. *Point of Arrival*

Check to be sure the length of the pitch does not exceed the length of the rappel rope doubled. Make sure that the arrival point leaves room for the party to assemble, for the recovery of the rope, and if need be, for a fresh *rappel.*

3. *Placing the Rappel*

The pull must be below the site of the *rappel.* If the rope is to pass directly over rock, smooth down the edges of the rock and see that the rope cannot slip off or jam. If a rope ring is used, it must be large enough to allow the rope, when recovered, to slip easily through it. If a piton is used, make sure it is firmly fixed and do not forget to add a ring or a karabiner.

4. *Throwing the Rappel*

Join the two extremities of the rope so as to be sure that the two halves are of equal length (the middle of the rope may be marked). Throw the rope in such a way that it does not catch on anything, and check to be certain that the two ends reach down to a proper landing site.

5. *Different Methods of Rappel Descent*

The two best methods are:

(a) *The "S" method:* The leading hand must not be clenched, it merely gives fore-and-aft balance. For braking, the rope is passed around the thigh and over the shoulder through the armpit. The rate of descent is controlled by the other hand.

(b) *Karabiner method:* Use two karabiners so as to avoid too sharp an angle in the rope. Descend slowly, especially if the rope is made of nylon. If you are roped up with climbing rope, keep it well clear, so that it does not foul the rappel rope.

6. *Recovery of the Rope*

The following procedure must be carried out if this is to be successful:

The first climber to come down must insure that the rope is slipping through easily.

The last climber must keep the two halves of the rope well apart. Once he is down, he pulls them away from each other to keep them separate. To recover the rope, he pulls on the half nearer the rock face on leaving the ring. He then draws the rope down smoothly, avoiding jerks, and making sure that the two halves do not foul each other.

Ice Technique

1. HANDLING THE ICE-AXE

As a walking stick: On gentle slopes, up to 25 degrees, use the ice-axe as a walking stick. On a traverse, keep it on the uphill side.

"Ramasse": On slopes of up to 45 degrees, the ice-axe is used in the "ramasse" position; that is to say, it is held horizontally; the point is embedded in the ice, one hand near the point pushing downwards, the other on the head, pushing uphill.

By this method, the ice-axe can be used for support and yet be ready to act as a brake on the slightest slip. It is most important to keep the pick of the ice-axe turned forwards, so as not to hurt yourself.

As an anchor: On steep slopes, more than 45 degrees, the pick of the ice-axe is driven into the ice at head level, the uphill hand on the head of the ice-axe, the other at the bottom of the handle.

2. USE OF CRAMPONS

Crampons make it possible to move rapidly, without cutting steps, up slopes of hard snow and *sérac* up to angles of 65 degrees, and up couloir ice, which is much harder, up to angles of 50 to 55 degrees. In other cases, steps must be cut. The two techniques of crampons and step-cutting are not generally used together, but are complementary. Either you use your crampons or you cut steps.

When wearing crampons, the ankles must be turned so that all the points of the crampons grip the snow or ice, however steep the slope may be. The position of the ice-axe is determined by the steepness of the slope.

3. CUTTING STEPS

Whenever you can, hold the ice-axe with both hands.

HORIZONTAL STEPS

A. In Sérac Ice:

First, outline the step in the ice. Next, cut away the ice above the step, working forwards from the back. Deepen the step by cutting away from the uphill side. Smooth the bearing surface of the step, making it slope slightly inwards. Rake the step with the blade of the ice-axe to clear away ice chips.

B. In Couloir Ice:

Above all, the ice must not be permitted to flake away. To insure this, first outline the site of the step with a few taps with the ice-axe struck perpendicularly to the slope. Carry on from there as for a step in *sérac* ice. The firmness of the step can be gauged by the sound. A hollow-sounding step is unsafe; the ice is on the point of flaking away.

"BENITIER" STEPS

These steps are used when climbing straight up steep ice. On both ascent and descent, they provide support to the tip of the foot. They are less comfortable than horizontal steps but are more quickly cut.

To cut a "*benitier*" step, two preliminary steps must be cut before the step at head level can be made. The ice-axe is wielded obliquely, alternately from the right and from the left.

HAND HOLDS

On very steep slopes, hand holds may also be cut, using the blade and then the point of the ice-axe.

4. ARTIFICIAL AIDS TO ICE CLIMBING

The use of artificial aids on ice is much less advanced than on rock.

Ice Pitons are fairly often used for security on slopes of poor quality ice, and in exceptional cases, for rope maneuvers.

Double Rope Climbing: In this method, the procedure is the same as on rock. It is used for crossing a *sérac* or bergschrund with vertical or overhanging walls.

The piton must be driven in perpendicularly to the direction of the strain it will have to bear. As in rock, the sound it gives out reveals whether the piton has broken up the ice.

Never pull on a piton along the axis of its insertion, for, depending on the quality of the ice, it might easily be pulled out.

Rappel descents may also be made using ice hummocks.

V. THE NEED FOR TECHNIQUE

Technique is more necessary in mountaineering than in many other sports, for in the mountains, the slightest mistake may cost you your life. In football, you may dislocate a bone; on skis, you may break a leg; but when climbing, if you fall, nine times out of ten you will be killed.

The hardest part of mountaineering is not the climbing itself, but remaining ever conscious of what you are doing when facing difficulty which may lead to danger, and especially remaining in control of your emotions.

Mountaineering demands such important physical qualities as strength, skill, suppleness, and endurance, but these are of no use if the climber has no head. A good runner is often said to "run with his head" before he runs with his legs. In climbing, this is supremely important.

If you use your head, your physical qualities will help you to acquire technique. Technique governs security, whether you are alone or in a party on a rope.

Technique is essential to offset danger. Mountaineering is not a perverse game between life and death. It is not a question of living dangerously, to use Nietzsche's words, but of living to the full in close kinship with nature and the elements. The idea of danger and the idea of difficulty are two completely different conceptions which are often muddled where mountaineering is concerned. The first is stupid, morbid and as much to be condemned as the other is healthy and virile.

That men in this age of easy living should be attracted by difficulty is a logical and just reaction. In contrast to the ordered world of towns, mountains offer the realm of the unknown. That is a delight which not even the oldest climbers can exhaust. But danger, that is quite another matter!

The real mountaineer does not like taking risks. It is

stupid to scorn death. We are too fond of life to gamble it away. In my profession of guide, I have to accept some risks every day. I know them too well, I fear them too much to like them or to seek them out. No, make sure you do the hardest and most daring things as safely as possible! The climber likes difficult pitches, even those which tax him to the utmost, but in such cases, it is as pleasant for him to feel safe, in his heart of hearts, as it is unpleasant to go beyond his resources, to run a risk or to incur some climbing hazard. Much too often have people considered mountaineering to be a more or less conscious form of trapeze work, in which the pleasure involved is in direct proportion to the risks incurred.

And yet the climber has sometimes to accept certain risks: the sudden onset of bad weather, storms, thunder, a hold which gives away although well tested, a couloir exposed to falling stones which must be rapidly crossed, a melting snowbridge which must be negotiated, a pitch which the climber suddenly finds is beyond him but from which he cannot withdraw, once he is committed. In all these cases, a thrill runs through him, but much too unpleasant a thrill for him to seek it out or to enjoy it. We are not "dicers with death."

It is not a question of being timid; the mountaineer has a certain courage, sometimes a certain audacity, but this courage and audacity must always be well considered and assessed. The climber must weigh on the one hand the difficulty to be mastered, and on the other his physical condition, his morale and his fatigue, and reach a conclusion soberly and without emotion. He can then assess whether there is any danger or whether he can safely carry on. For this, he must *know himself.* He must be capable of summing things up accurately.

Thorough knowledge of one's own capacity is the first great difficulty in the practice of mountaineering. This is more important than climbing problems, more important than technique. This knowledge is also a marvelous reward to be earned in this sport in which cheating is out of the question and in which the individual's judgment is not influenced by spectators or by crowds. Man is alone, upheld by his will and his enthusiasm, face to face with rocks, ice and the elements. There is no way around this pure and straightforward encounter.

With the object of attaining this self-knowledge, each climb may be considered as a test, though this need not detract from the appreciative and esthetic side of climbing.

You may, therefore, like to keep a climbing log, in which you can record the following:

Date
Peak climbed, and height
Route followed
Weather conditions
Mountain conditions and difficulties encountered
Composition of the party.

You might go further and rate your own performance from the following standpoints:

Skill on rock
Skill on ice
Feeling for the route followed
Security and rope handling
Calmness, authority and decision
Physical resources.

These ratings will necessarily be arbitrary; try, however to be fair and to remain objective. For example, I imagine that the mark you will award yourself for rope handling will not always be 100 per cent; did you not leave the rope lying about on the snow? Were your decisions the best ones possible? Did you not hesitate about the route? Did you not go wrong once or twice?

You might also try to award marks to your companions, quite objectively.

In the mountains, you must know yourself well, but you must know your companions equally well.

You are going to undertake climbs with a guide or with a competent and experienced friend. Your aim will be not only to reach a peak by following a leader more or less easily, but also to examine, question, experiment, and interpret everything, to draw a climbing lesson from it and so to become a mountaineer.

VI. A CLIMB IS CHOSEN, THEN PREPARED

It is essential that the projected climb should be within your physical capacity. Do not choose too hard a climb. You would labor in vain and perhaps abandon a magnificent sport in discouragement. In any case, the pleasure and profit you would draw from the climbing would be diminished, besides risking an accident.

Preparing for and planning a climb is very pleasant. Quite apart from your physical condition, maintained by physical training, walking and climbing practice, you must study the climb you are planning. You must know each climb intimately before actually making it; that is, have clearly in mind the situation of the summit and of the route to be followed, as well as other routes; and be accurately informed as to the state of the mountain. You must assess the conditions, find out what the difficulties are, and in some cases what the dangers are—for example, falling stones at such-and-such a time at such-and-such a spot. You must know where warm, cold or ice-covered rock will be encountered, according to its exposure. The success of the longest climbs depends on the accumulation of small details, carefully studied.

This preparation can be carried out in various ways: by map reading, studying guidebooks, mountain books, accounts of climbs, technical notes, and photographs which have appeared in climbing magazines. (There is a great difference between merely looking at a photograph and really interpreting it.) You can question friends who have done the climbs. When I knew mountains but little, I remember spending whole days studying a massif. What plans! What dreams! Reading a map is a thrilling pastime.

You must keep in good training for walking, otherwise your thighs will get tired in descending moraines. And practice climbing, both on rock and on ice, as often as you can.

VII. THE CLIMB

It is often useful, for certain climbs, to reconnoiter the day before the terrain you will have to cover in darkness the following day.

Prepare your climbing equipment the day before, and carefully sort out those items which are to remain at the hut.

Draw up a timetable and try to keep to it.

You will seldom regret starting off too early; you will always regret starting off too late.

You must reach the summit early and keep a large margin of time for security.

You must know how to travel fast, if need be; that is, without losing any time. This can be done especially by two methods:

First, by all the members of the rope climbing together, on easy terrain, without letting the rope drag, the climbers holding the coiled rope firmly in their hands.

Secondly, by means of rope maneuvers (and on occasion rucksack maneuvers) when one climber goes up at a time.

You must not waste time on the way up, so as to be able to make a pause at the top sufficient for a good rest before coming down, and also for enjoying the view spread out before your eyes. Perhaps the greatest thing to be said for technique is that it makes for contemplation, by eliminating fatigue. We go climbing for many reasons, one of which is surely to contemplate and admire. A climber who is weary through lack of technique cannot relax completely and look around; he is worried and apt to be in a hurry.

Eat little and often.

Bear the condition of the snow in mind when drawing up the timetable for the descent. Some pitches, the Whymper couloir on the Aiguille Verte, for example, although perfectly safe before the sun has reached them, become very dangerous in the heat of the day.

The faster you climb, the safer, especially on long climbs which last two or three days. But even on one-day climbs, never forget that weather and other conditions can change suddenly at great heights. It is quite unacceptable—excepting on long climbs over ice—to come in from a climb three or four hours late.

Throughout the whole excursion, you must interpret the mountain; for example, you must put your crampons on when you need them, and not when the technical notes tell you to. All that depends so much on conditions which vary from year to year! You must try to make the climb a personal achievement.

It is important to know when and where in the climb the difficult pitches occur, so as to be ready to tackle them. Thanks to the classification of difficult pitches, you can acquire fairly accurate information on the difficulties when the rock is dry. Such classification claims to do one thing only: to facilitate the editing of technical notes and guidebooks. Whereas formerly a pitch was said to be difficult, fairly difficult, very difficult, hard, tricky, dangerous, exposed, etc., it is now said to be of the third or fifth degree. This guidance is more precise, though still not perfect, and permits comparisons to be drawn with pitches which have been previously climbed.

This system of classification applies necessarily to dry rock.

A pitch can be classified, but this is not possible for a whole climb, unless the degree of difficulty is the same the whole way up. Modern classification of pitches can therefore be useful and can be recommended, but it must be used with caution.

VIII. THE BROTHERHOOD OF THE ROPE

Never hesitate, during the climb, to ask the friend or guide who is with you to let you lead the rope from time to time. This will give you responsibility and build up your confidence, and will be excellent for your mountaineering education. Yet one seldom or never sees a client climbing in front of his guide. People have a fixed idea of what a guide is: a professional, who, in return for a certain sum of money, takes you to the summit to which you aspire. But the guide is more than that: he is a competent friend who controls the party, but who also teaches you and stimulates your interest. "There is only one real luxury, that of human relationships," Saint Exupéry has written. Mountains offer one of the finest frameworks in which these can develop. Your climbing companion is the man with whom you will share the good and exacting moments of mountaineering, and many of your finest experiences. The choice of companion is as important as the choice of climb.

Through such apprenticeship to technique, through advice such as this, I have found you all, my Good Companions of Adventure.

I am immensely happy, for I have felt the rope between us. We are linked for life. We have approached the stars together and at such heights, the air has a special savor.

What a strange situation we are in, as seen by a layman—two beings united by a thread between heaven and earth! When I start climbing again, the reason for climbing is at once clear to me, or one of the reasons—to struggle on for nothing else but satisfaction. Here the significance of the struggle is to strip men, so as better to bring them together.

Together we have sweated on the moraines and shivered in the bivouacs, the sun has warmed us, then scorched us, the wind has caressed us, then buffeted us. We have been scraped by granite walls and our knees have been grazed by stones and boulders. We have slept on boards and sometimes on snow, waiting for the first hint of dawn and the return of the sun, we have labored down endless *rappels* on wet ropes which clung to our damp clothes. We have been mocked, scorned and battered by the elemental storms.

Together we have known apprehension, uncertainty and fear; but of what importance is all that? For it was only up there that we discovered many things of which we had previously known nothing: a joy that was new to us, happiness that was doubled because it was shared, a wordless friendship which was no mere superficial impulse.

We felt at once that our ordinary lives and their pleasures no longer satisfied us, and as we came down towards the plains, nostalgia for the heights grew in us.

But I am happy again, because I have found you all again during this apprenticeship to technique. Here, I am standing on Jean's shoulder; there, Maurice shared a lemon with me; on the *arête* Edouard is pulling down the *rappel* rope; on the ice slope, Henri taught me to cut steps. You, Henri, above all; you may count for nothing in the eyes of many, but for me, you are my "Elder Brother of the Mountains."

I wish all climbers an Elder Brother who can always be looked up to with love and respect, who will watch the way you rope yourself up, and who, as he initiates you into an exacting life, looks after you like a mother hen.

The one who shares with you his fleeting sovereignty at 12,000 feet and who points out the surrounding peaks as a gardener shows his flowers.

The one at whom we all gaze with envy, for the mountain hut is his lodging and the mountain his domain.

The friendship of a man as rich as that cannot be bought.

Such friendships and such experiences appear again and again in the adventures in climbing the great north faces of the Alps described in this book.

APPENDIX: GEOGRAPHICAL AND HISTORICAL INFORMATION ON THE GREAT NORTH FACES OF THE ALPS

THE NORTH FACE OF THE GRANDES JORASSES

Mont Blanc (15,781 feet), the highest mountain in Europe, is surrounded by satellites which are giants in their own right. Of these one of the noblest is the Grandes Jorasses (13,800 feet), which lies six miles east of Mont Blanc's summit itself. It is really a great ridge, having many points along it, of which the easternmost, or

This information was included in the original English-language edition of *Starlight and Storm* and was written by the translators, Wilfrid Noyce and Sir John Hunt.

Pointe Walker, is the true summit. This ridge forms part of the frontier between Italy and France. The northern or French side drops in one mighty plunge to the Leschaux glacier 4,000 feet below. It forms the north face described here. The southern or Italian side is sunny and at a much more easy angle, and it was up this that the first ascents were made, by Horace Walker (1868), Edward Whymper, and many others. The pioneers did not, as was the case with most great peaks, go first along the ridges, for here these are more difficult. It was not till 1911 that G. Winthrop Young, with Josef Knubel as guide, succeeded in climbing the west ridge, from the Col des Grandes Jorasses, and in the same month descended the east ridge to the Col des Hirondelles. The east ridge was not ascended till 1927.

After the ridges came the faces. In this chapter Rébuffat describes the north face of the Grandes Jorasses below its highest point, the Pointe Walker. Attempted many times by the best climbers of the day, the Pointe Walker defeated them all until climbed in 1938 by Italians who had practiced the latest techniques in the Dolomites.

By way of background it should be explained that mountaineers had begun to explore Alpine peaks by their faces before World War I. After it they were climbing more often without guides, and were turning more and more for their new ground to the great faces of rock, snow, and ice enclosed by the ridges which had hitherto been the usual way up mountains. This was natural enough, for men have the urge for what is unexplored. Thus already before 1914 the faces had yielded fine climbing of the older style (those of the Weisshorn pioneered by G. Winthrop Young are a case in point). Now steeper and steeper walls were attempted, with the added risks which face climbing involves. On a ridge, with drops on either hand, it is not usually possible for stone or snow avalanches to descend on the climber. But a face, seamed as it is by snow gullies called couloirs, offers natural chutes for these when they are loosened by the action of sun and frost. Sometimes they are avoidable on ribs protruding as minor ridges. Sometimes the danger must be accepted as an inherent objective risk which no mountaineering skill can offset.

With the development, particularly by the Germans and Italians, of a "piton technique," climbers began to scale ever-steeper precipices. Whereas normally the climber depends for hold on the grip of fingers and toes in the rock's roughness, and for safety on rock projections round which he can tie the rope, now it was found that by hammering in these iron pegs or pitons, and threading his rope through snap-rings known as "karabiners," he could climb walls of rock devoid of any natural hold at all. He did not, as before, depend on balance. Concurrently the art was developed of bivouacking in slings suspended from the rock, since the greater faces described in this book could not be climbed in a day.

THE NORTH-EAST FACE OF PIZ BADILE

The Engadine in southeast Switzerland is a valley sixty miles long running northeast from the Italian frontier north of Lake Como, and watered by the River Inn. The centers of Pontresina and St. Moritz are very popular tourist resorts, for the valleys with their woods are as lovely as the snows, and the district is also a health resort.

The highest group of mountains in this district includes the Piz Bernina (13,288 feet), the Piz Roseg (12,917 feet), and the Piz Palü (12,812 feet). These are snow mountains, and it is some way to the east of them, up the wild Bondasca Valley, that the Piz Badile and its peers, the Piz Cengalo and Pizzi Gemelli, lie. They are rock mountains, not so high as the Bernina group (Piz Badile is 10,853 feet), but sliced in great sweeps of firm granite rock that give some exceptionally difficult climbing.

THE NORTH FACE OF THE DRUS

The Mer de Glace is a glacier, a great river of ice winding down from the higher snows of Mont Blanc, past the Grandes Jorasses towards the Valley of Chamonix. Above the true right bank, in its lower reaches, the two Aiguilles du Dru (12,320 and 12,248 feet) stand as a tapering gray pyramid staring down at the Montenvers, the large hotel and belvedere on the other side (6,267 feet), to which the rack-railway climbs from Chamonix. Here countless tourists come, to gaze or walk upon the Mer de Glace.

Since its first ascent in 1879 the lesser Dru has always been considered the hardest peak of the Alps by its *route normale*. This route is the scene of a part of R. Frison-Roche's well-known novel *First on the Rope*.

It is interesting that in this chapter Gaston Rébuffat noted the possibility of the west face when he climbed the north face. Since the ascent of the latter it has been the former, to the right of and conspicuous from the Montenvers, that has attracted attention. The first ascent in 1952, in which many pitons were used, took Guido Magnone's party eight days. They did it in two phases. First of all four days, retreat and rest, then up the north face to a point level with that reached before. Then a day to traverse to that point by using expansion-bolts on holdless rock. The summit next day, bivouac, and down the following morning. On the second ascent one member of the French party died on the way down after a severe ordeal. The third ascent was made in 1954 by the brilliant English climbers J. Brown and D. Whillans in a day and a half.

THE MATTERHORN

The Matterhorn, or in French le Cervin, 14,780 feet high, is one of the highest peaks of the Pennine Alps in the district known as the Valais. Others are Monte Rosa

(15,200 feet), the Weisshorn (14,804 feet), and the Dom (14,942 feet). Isolated from these the Matterhorn stands up, an immense tower or tooth of rock, on the frontier of Switzerland and Italy. It has four ridges converging on the summit: the north or Hörnli ridge in Switzerland, by which the mountain was first climbed; the Italian ridge to the south, coming up to the Italian summit which is a few feet lower than the Swiss; to the west the great curving Zmutt ridge; and to the east the Furggen, formidably sharp and steep at its top.

Everybody knows the story of Edward Whymper's first ascent of the Matterhorn by the Swiss ridge in 1865, and the tragedy of the descent, when four members of the party fell to their death down the north face.[1] A few days later Jean-Antoine Carrel, the Italian guide, made the first ascent of the Italian ridge. In the years that followed, the great days of guided climbing, the Zmutt ridge was pioneered by A. F. Mummery and his guides in 1879. It remains one of the great Alpine routes of the old style. The Furggen was climbed fairly early up to the shoulder below its steep final section, but not

---

[1]The classic account of this climb and accident is given in Whymper's *Scrambles Amongst the Alps* (1900).

completed till 1911 by M. Piacenza with the guides Jean-Joseph Carrel and Joseph Gaspard.

The climbing of the faces followed that of the ridges, as recounted earlier. On most mountains it became possible to climb very steep walls with the aid of pitons, which afforded security and also enabled the climbers to assist themselves up holdless and overhanging passages. With the Matterhorn it is security that is needed rather than the overcoming of impossible steepness; the chief dangers are the objective ones of falling stones and rotten rock; pitons do not hold firmly. The first ascent of this very difficult and usually dangerous north face is given briefly here.

In recent years, by judging to a nicety the conditions of the mountain and waiting for the right moment, parties have been able to climb the face in one day without bivouacking on the way up. But it remains an undertaking of the first magnitude, partly because of the sudden storms which strike the mountain in its isolated position, and also because of the indeterminate character of the face and the looseness of the rock. Stones sweep constantly down the gullies, some through natural causes, some dislodged by parties climbing up or down the

Swiss ridge. Furthermore, as has been said, it is not possible for a party to secure its ascent by using pitons because of the friable rock, which will not hold firm. Parties are therefore likely to follow different lines. It is perhaps for this reason that a famous guide has given his opinion that of all the major north faces the Matterhorn will continue longest to be considered of great severity.

THE CIMA GRANDE DI LAVAREDO

The Dolomite Alps lie between the Adige and Isarco valleys of north Italy (Italian since 1918), south of the Brenner Pass. The geological composition of the limestone results in the extraordinary formations of vertical tower and pinnacle for which the district is famous. It is not, however, as thoroughly known to British climbers as the greater Alps. This is partly because of the distance, since these are among the farthest peaks for us to reach, partly because, since there is rock in Britain but no eternal snow, many climbers going abroad tend to seek out the glaciers.

Those who do go, however, find as rich reward in the

flowers and woods as in the fantastic shapes that spring from them. The names of a number of well-known British climbers are associated with the first ascents of peaks in the Dolomites. In general the climbing tends to be of great steepness, but on the ordinary routes it is provided with a corresponding abundance of holds. Snow is almost always absent and rubber- or rope-soled shoes are therefore extensively used. The climbs are long but do not demand early starts.

The sheer, holdless sides of the peaks have also been yielding one by one to the climber, thanks to an engineering technique which can overcome any rock surface, however steep. Of such is the Cima Grande.

THE NORTH FACE OF THE EIGER

The Eiger (or Ogre), 13,040 feet high, is the last bastion of the chain of Bernese Oberland mountains overlooking the Grindelwald valley to the north. In many ways it is the most striking of all. Seen from Berne, from the Lake of Thun or, nearer, from the winter sports resort of

Mürren, it appears as the left-hand peak of a trinity with the Mönch (Monk, 13,463 feet) and the Jungfrau (Maiden, 13,641 feet); it is a gigantic tooth whose left-hand edge has been sliced away to form the awesome precipice, over 5,000 feet high, which overhangs the meadows of Grindelwald. This great slice is, in fact, the abrupt end of the Oberland range on the northern side.

Thus situated, the mountain has long been familiar to tourists, skiers and mountaineers, as well as to the people of the Oberland. The first ascent, by the easy, broken flank which bounds the face on the right, was made in 1858. It is the only easy route. The right-hand ridge rises from the Eigerjoch, a saddle between the Eiger and Mönch very difficult of access. The other important ridge, the Mitteleggi, which bounds the face on the left, was ascended only in 1921 by the Japanese Juko Maki with Grindelwald guides. It is said that a long pole was used to overcome the obstacles where ropes are now fixed. Between the ridge and the climb described in this chapter a route, difficult but not excessively so, was worked out in 1932. The story of the great face proper does not begin until 1935.

The Eiger is notorious as a magnet for violent storms, partly because of its situation between the Oberland snow fields and the low valleys. These storms, and the snow and rock avalanches which fall down its north face, make this exceedingly difficult climb a hazardous adventure as well.

GLOSSARY

Abseil, see rappel.

Aiguille, needle or sharp peak of rock.

Arête, narrow ridge of rock or snow.

Belay, the rope hitched round a rock projection or attached to a piton (q.v.), thus securing the climber to the mountain.

Bergschrund (or *rimaye*), a large crevasse separating the upper slopes of a glacier from the steeper slopes of rock or ice above.

Chimney, a narrow, vertical rock cleft. Usually the climber wedges his body, feet against one wall, back against

the other. This is the technique known as "chimneying."

Col, depression or saddle between peaks in a mountain
chain.

Corner, usually a right angle, like the corner of a room, in
a rock wall. In the angle itself there is nearly always
a crack.

Couloir, gully or furrow in the mountainside, usually
snow-filled.

Crampon, metal frame with spikes, fitting the sole of the
boot. For use on hard snow or ice. Crampons are
strapped on to the boot.

Crevasse, fissure in surface of a glacier, often very deep.

Espadrille (or *kletterschuh*), light shoe, rope-, felt-, or
rubber-soled, worn for difficult rock-climbing.
They are more adhesive, pleasanter and safer
than boots.

Friable, tending to crumble. Used of rock.

Glacier, large river of ice and snow winding between
mountain walls. Glaciers are fringed by the débris
of stones and earth scoured from the mountain-
sides as the ice shifts downwards. This débris is
known as moraine.

Glissade, the art of sliding down a snow slope, usually standing upright with the axe used as a brake.

Ice-axe, usually about 3½ feet long, it has a head with a pick on one side for step-cutting in ice, a blade on the other for clearing snow or ice-chips. At the other end is a spike, useful when the axe is used as a walking-stick.

Karabiner (or *mousqueton*), snap-ring attached to piton, so that the rope can be passed through it.

Kletterschuh, see espadrille.

Moraine, see glacier.

Mousqueton, see karabiner.

Pitch, stretch of difficult ice or rock between ledges or stances. The pitch is climbed by one climber while the other is secured to rock or piton.

Piton, iron peg sharp at one end with a hole at the other for the karabiner. The piton is driven into a crack in the rock; it can then be used either to raise the climber to its level by the second climber pulling on a special rope threaded through the karabiner, or to secure the party, the climbing rope being threaded through in the same way.

Rappel (or *abseil*), the rope doubled round a projection or piton. Taking the doubled rope in his hands and winding it over his shoulder, etc., the climber can quickly descend vertical or overhanging rocks.

Rimaye, see bergschrund.

Scree, slopes of small loose stones, the débris fallen from cliffs above.

Sérac, tower composed of ice, between the crevasses of a glacier.

Stance, ledge or other position in which one climber can stand and secure the rope while the other climbs.

Traverse, crossing of a rope horizontally or diagonally.

Verglas, ice covering rock, a highly treacherous problem on a difficult rock-climb.

Vibram, treaded rubber sole of a climbing boot.

A Note on the Type

The principal text of this Modern Library edition
was set in a digitized version of Janson, a typeface that dates
from about 1690 and was cut by Nicholas Kis, a Hungarian
working in Amsterdam. The original matrices have survived
and are held by the Stempel foundry in Germany.
Hermann Zapf redesigned some of the weights and sizes
for Stempel, basing his revisions on the original design.